IN THE STEPS OF STANLEY

By the same author

Where the Trails Run Out

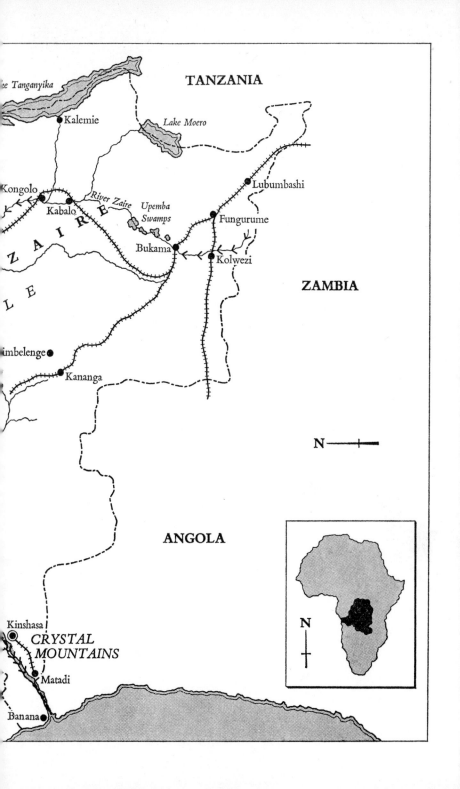

JOHN BLASHFORD-SNELL

In the Steps of Stanley

Hutchinson of London

Hutchinson & Co (Publishers) Ltd
3 Fitzroy Square, London W1

London Melbourne Sydney Auckland
Wellington Johannesburg and agencies
throughout the world

First published 1975
© The Scientific Exploration Society 1975

Extracts from *The Exploration Diaries of H. M. Stanley*
© William Kimber & Co Ltd 1961

Set in Monotype Garamond

Printed in Great Britain by The Anchor Press Ltd
and bound by Wm Brendon & Son Ltd
both of Tiptree, Essex

ISBN 0 09 125080 3

This book is dedicated to

MR WALTER H. ANNENBERG

who

while American Ambassador to the
Court of St James did so much to
assist the Zaire River Expedition and
to bring together the servicemen,
scientists and explorers of Britain,
the United States of America and the
Republic of Zaire.

Contents

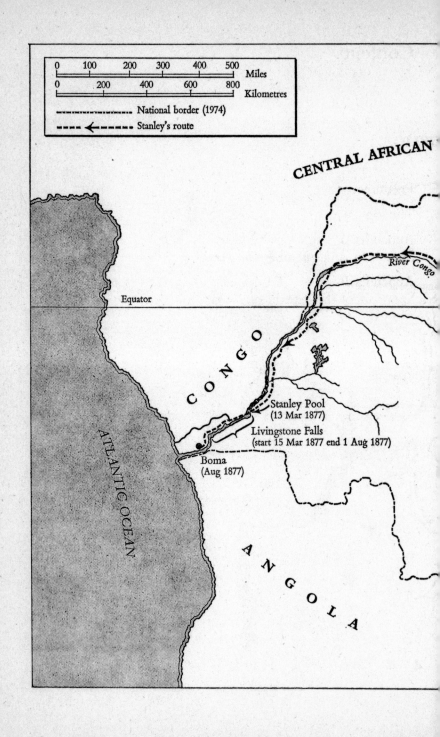

0 100 200 300 400 500 Miles
0 200 400 600 800 Kilometres

National border (1974)
← Stanley's route

CENTRAL AFRICAN

River Congo

Equator

C O N G O

Stanley Pool
(13 Mar 1877)

Livingstone Falls
(start 15 Mar 1877 end 1 Aug 1877)

Boma
(Aug 1877)

ATLANTIC OCEAN

A N G O L A

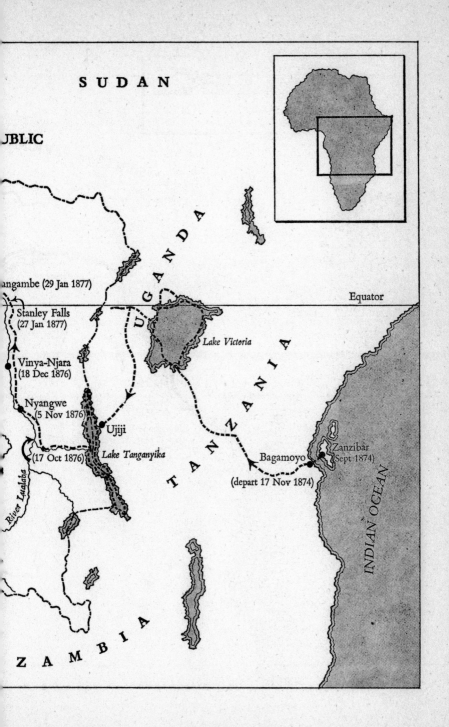

SUDAN

JBLIC

Equator

angambe (29 Jan 1877)

Stanley Falls
(27 Jan 1877)

Vinya-Njara
(18 Dec 1876)

Nyangwe
(5 Nov 1876)

Ujiji

(17 Oct 1876)

Lake Tanganyika

River Lualaba

U G A N D A

Lake Victoria

T A N Z A N I A

Bagamoyo

(depart 17 Nov 1874)

Zanzibar
Sept 1874)

I N D I A N   O C E A N

Z A M B I A

Illustrations

David Gestetner at the moment of impact with the rock ledge

Portaging *La Vision* at Yalala

The Edwin Arnold Falls with Jet 2 in foreground (*Mannering and Associates, NZ*)

Jon Hamilton takes Jet 1 through a moderate rapid (*Mannering and Associates, NZ*)

Barclays Bank heads out into the Atlantic

At the Presidency with President Mobutu Seso Seko

Thanksgiving service at sunset on Sunday, 19 January

Preamble

'Doctor Livingstone, I presume?' These immortal words, uttered by Henry Morton Stanley, heralded a great chapter in the annals of exploration.

Livingstone, that remarkable Scot, had been found by an already successful journalist who was to become equally as famous as a dogged, determined and ruthless explorer. Their meeting was indeed an historic occasion, which made a deep impression on Stanley, and during the four months he spent with Livingstone he learned much of the old missionary's discoveries hopes and theories.

When in 1874 he learned of the good doctor's death, Stanley immediately said, 'May I be selected to succeed him in opening up Africa to the shining light of Christianity.' His chief ambition was to pursue Livingstone's last unfinished quest on which he had died, the quest for the source of the Nile. We now know that John Hanning Speke had in fact found the principal source at the Ripon Falls on the northern shore of Lake Victoria in 1862, but twelve years later the authenticity of Speke's discovery was still disputed by many of his contemporaries. Livingstone was among them, and he believed that the Lualaba River which he had found to the west of Lake Tanganyika might itself possibly be the Nile. The only way to test his theory was to follow the Lualaba's course, and Stanley resolved to do just this. Backed by *The Daily Telegraph* of London and the *New York Herald*, he set out from Zanzibar in November 1874 with three other white men and 356 Africans, carrying an impressive quantity of weapons and a sectionalized wooden boat which he named *Lady Alice* after his fiancée, a Miss

Alice Pike of New York. He kept a daily diary of his travels, and in the entry for 17 November 1874 he defines his enterprise as the Anglo-American Expedition for the Discovery of the Nile and Congo Sources. He was in fact to cross the 'Dark Continent' from east to west.

Throughout 1875 the expedition pressed on across Africa, circumnavigating and surveying the Great Lakes, driving off attacks by hostile tribes and marching, marching, marching. Little was known about the interior of Africa at this time, and in matters of detail the available maps could be compared with those of the moon's surface today. In October 1876, however, Stanley and his now severely depleted party reached the banks of the Lualaba at Nyangwe. Here his route joined with that of the Zaire River Expedition in 1974–75, which began its journey as near as possible to the source some nine hundred kilometres south of this point and thus covered a very long stretch that Stanley never saw. The Lualaba is not, of course, any part of the Nile but the headstream of the Congo. Together they form the mighty confluence which flows across Central Africa to the Atlantic and is today known as the Zaire River.

Stanley finally reached the Atlantic coast in August 1877. Two years later he again returned to Central Africa to play an important role in establishing what became recognized in 1885 as the Congo Free State. This was formally annexed by Belgium in 1908 as the Belgian Congo, and in 1960 it achieved independence as the Democratic Republic of the Congo. Finally, in 1971 and after many internal vicissitudes, both the republic and its great river were given their present name of Zaire. It is in fact an old name, known to Europeans since the fifteenth century and derived from a Kikongo word which just means 'river'. 'Congo' is first encountered in the seventeenth century, being taken from the kingdom of Kongo which adjoined the river's lower course.

No detailed scientific work was carried out on Stanley's expedition, and in the years that followed the vast Congo Basin (as it is still internationally known) remained largely cloaked in dense tropical jungle and relatively inaccessible. Then in 1970 it was suggested that the Scientific Exploration Society, the international cadre of explorers and scientists, should attempt to carry out a programme of medical and scientific research. It was obvious that with few roads in the area, the best way would be to move by river, traversing most of the 4300 kilometres of these dangerous and rapid-strewn waters, much of which had not previously been navigated. I was chosen to lead the expedition, which was to set forth in 1974 and thus also commemorate the centenary of Stanley's journey.

The late Prince William of Gloucester, who had hoped to accompany us, launched the expedition at a dinner given in London on the hundreth anniversary of Stanley's famous meeting with Livingstone. A committee was formed under the chairmanship of Major-General Griff Caldwell to direct overall policy and raise money. In December 1971 Captain Martin Romilly, Royal Anglian Regiment, and the historian and veteran explorer Richard Snailham flew out to Zaire to carry out a detailed reconnaissance.

My first major task was to select my team and its equipment. Initially, I envisaged a small team of approximately forty people to support the large group of scientists who would be so essential to our main purpose. Our early studies of the area, however, showed that the sheer scale of the country and its river would require a much bigger expedition. The Zaire is the seventh longest river in the world and the second biggest in its outflow, which averages 42 000 cubic metres per second. The Republic of Zaire is the third largest country in Africa, approximately the size of Western Europe, and it has one of the highest rainfall areas in the world. So my team expanded, eventually reaching a total strength of 165 members, including fifty scientists and nine women. We drew our members from all over the world, selecting them mainly for their compatability and industry. People with experience of Africa and those with a knowledge of French or the local languages were especially sought after. Our final complement included Americans, Australians, Belgians, Britons, Canadians, Fijians, Frenchmen, Nepalese, New Zealanders, and a Dane. We also asked for a strong contingent of Zairois servicemen and scientists.

I was particularly fortunate to secure as my personal assistant a charming nurse who had worked in Zaire and spoke fluent French. Miss Pamela Baker, SRN, is the daughter of George Baker, one of our earliest supporters, who as Head of Chancery at the British Embassy in the Zaire capital of Kinshasa (formerly called Leopoldville) did much to help our reconnaissance team.

In London our old friend Kay Thompson and her daughter Jill Henderson organized the expedition office, while Colonel Bruce Maude and Michael Hooker Associates Limited tackled the daunting task of raising £120 000 in cash and kind. Among our leading supporters was the then American Ambassador in London. His Excellency, Mr Walter Annenberg, ever a man to encourage Anglo-American relations, also had the vision to see that this undertaking could achieve much in the cause of science.

Among those who joined us as key members of our force was ex-Royal Marine Captain Mike Gambier whom I had known for many years and now asked to act as my deputy. Major Derek Jackson became commander of the logistic support group, with Major Gordon Mitchell of the Scots Guards as quartermaster. A tough and experienced sapper, Major Ernie Durey, was to run the engineer section. As my right-hand man and intelligence officer, I appointed Captain Peter Marett, RE, who played this same role on our previous expedition to the Darien Gap. Advance liaison in Zaire was assigned to my old friend Major Tom Hawkins, RE, and his able assistant WO 1 Jim Winter. Major Ashley Barker (R. Signals) was given the task of co-ordinating the administration of the scientific team. This included a galaxy of experts with Mr Frederick Rodger, MD, MCH, FRCS(G), DOMS, FRGS, a leading 'authority on tropical eye disease, leading the medical research group in their search for a cure for river blindness.

To build boats that would negotiate the raging rapids, which were said to have waves up to twelve metres high, we went to Ron Smith, the famous river runner on the Colorado. After talking with us and examining our reconnaissance film, Ron produced three giant inflatable rafts that could be collapsed and portaged (carried overland) when inevitably we met impassable cataracts or waterfalls. Much depended on water-level, and so we selected the period of October to February as the time when the higher level would be most suitable. For the really narrow upper stretches of the river we chose Avon Professional inflatables, and throughout the expedition we were to use Avon S400 inflatables for reconnaissance. His Royal Highness Prince Philip suggested we consider using water jet craft, and after a trial two 200 hp Hamilton Jets were shipped to Africa.

Many of the lessons we had learned when exploring the Blue Nile in 1968 were remembered, and it was a great advantage having some of the old team with us again. No effort was indeed spared to ensure our craft were the best available, though in terms of experiment no really suitable river could be found to compare with the Zaire and no rapids to match her cataracts. So in the end we could only hope and pray that our choice was right. Our lives would depend on it!

Air support was another vital factor. Here we were fortunate to obtain the assistance of the British Army Air Corps, who provided a single-engine Beaver light aircraft which eventually flew out to Africa on its own, crossing the Sahara on its way to Zaire.

Nineteen-seventy-four was not a good year in which to launch one of the most ambitious expeditions ever undertaken. Money was, to say the least, hard to find, and even as I write we are still paying the bills! Civil air-charter rates were soaring. The price of petrol was rising daily, as was the cost of almost everything else. Hard-pressed British Army units could ill-afford to spare good men. In Africa political feelings were running high. The wind of change was sweeping through Angola and Mozambique. Nevertheless, we believed it *could* be done. Supported and encouraged by the British Ministry of Defence, the Explorers' Club in New York, *The Daily Telegraph*, Anglia-Survival Television, plus a great many other commerical concerns, we went on planning.

A list of all our major sponsors is given in Appendix B. It is difficult to single out individual companies, but I feel it is only right I should mention Gestetner who backed us to the hilt and in whose honour one of the giant inflatable craft was named *David Gestetner*. We are similarly grateful for the valuable and generous support of Barclays International for whom another giant inflatable was named *Barclays Bank*, and yet again to John Tucker who, with Gordon Gamble of the Jersey branch of the Royal Trust Company of Canada, helped us to organize the sponsorship of young people which has already inspired others to assist young explorers. One or two firms who helped Stanley also helped us, including the British India Steam Navigation Company who transported him to Zanzibar in 1874.

The text of *In the Steps of Stanley* consists chiefly of my official log written daily as our journey progressed, and is not designed to be the complete story of the expedition; that is being written separately by Richard Snailham. Some parts of the log were recorded by my deputy, Mike Gambier, and Richard Snailham himself made several entries. Much was dictated by torchlight to my long-suffering PA, Pamela Baker, who took it down in abbreviated freehand; her only reward being a sip of J & B whisky to revive her from time to time! Such a log can of its very nature have few literary pretensions, but I hope that by leaving it largely unembellished I may have preserved with a greater sense of immediacy something of what we experienced and how it all felt at the time. I am not qualified to discuss the scientific programme which was our prime concern throughout, and my log entries on these subjects are essentially those of a layman.

The extracts from H. M. Stanley's diaries have been interpolated at points where our journeys coincide, so as to provide an appropriate historical contrast. The very existence of these diaries only became known in 1960, and they were first published the following year as *The Exploration Diaries of H. M. Stanley*, edited by Richard Stanley and Alan Neame. I am indebted to the publishers, William Kimber and Company, for permission to quote them so extensively here. Wherever they appear throughout the text they have been set in smaller type, with the date heading given as, for example, *October 17th*, as distinct from the formula of *Thursday 17 October* in bold type used at the beginning of each of my own log entries.

My thanks are due to Peter Marett for checking the manuscript and for preparing the maps which make such a valuable contribution to the book. In addition I wish to thank the editor of *The Daily Telegraph* for the use of many photographs taken by Kenneth Mason and reproduced in this book. I am also extremely grateful to Mr Richard Stanley for all his encouragement and advice to the expedition. Having traversed the same river, I can say in all honesty that I am full of admiration for his grandfather's courage, determination and utter selflessness. If we have even approached his example, we may be well satisfied.

The Log

Friday 4 October 1974

At 0900 hours the giant DC 10 of Air Zaire thundered off the runway at Gatwick Airport. We were soon rising through the low cloud and drizzle. After the usual last-minute rush of final preparation the expedition was under way. Sitting at the front of the massive airliner with my tactical headquarters (Tac HQ) we took a gulp of very welcome iced champagne and held our first 'orders group of' the expedition. The flight was quite superb and easily the best I have ever experienced anywhere in the world. Food and wine flowed and the service was carried out efficiently by Zairois hostesses.

Arrived Kinshasa (formerly Leopoldville) 1630 hours. Met by Captain Paul Turner, Queen's Own Hussars, and Captain Mike Heathcote, Royal Marines, our advance party. Local press and TV in evidence. Some twenty liaison officers (LOs) and numerous items of freight joined us at this point. Included in freight was a small yellow buggy. This is a six-wheel, two-man, amphibious vehicle that is said to be able to cross almost any terrain on earth! It has been presented by the Atrima Company. Temperature warm, humidity rising. Flight continued through early evening and we landed at Lubumbashi (formerly Elisabethville) at 1930 hours. Met by Major Derek Jackson and Major Tom Hawkins. Quite a reception. Committed a slight *faux pas* myself on leaving aircraft. At foot of steps was attractive local lady whom I concluded to be part of reception committee. She was first to shake hands with me and we exchanged effusive greetings in French. Derek intervened, whispering in my ear that the 'local lady' was there for quite a different reason!

Following reception, aircraft unloaded by Zaire Army and ourselves on to waiting trucks. Throughout a humid African night we toiled on swampy airfield unhindered by any customs or immigration! The scene reminiscent of an Ian Fleming thriller. Eventually all trucks loaded and convoy lumbered off towards Kolwezi. Long slow drive, dusty road, a few animals. Arrived shortly before dawn.

Saturday 5 October

Expedition continued to arrive at dawn, and after short sleep unpacking commenced. Carried out inspection at midday and formally met all LOs. Presented them with Polaroid sunglasses which they seemed to appreciate. Our advance party under Derek Jackson has got all the arrangements for our arrival and reception very well in hand.

Dinner with Victor Forrest, local Belgian businessman. Very pleasant and temperature not too hot. In honour of all his assistance to us decided to name one of our boats *Malta Forrest*, after his recently deceased father, currently in the local deep freeze, awaiting transportation to Belgium for burial.

The Reverend Basil Pratt, our chaplain, held a short service tonight.

Sunday 6 October

Studied reconnaissance report by Dr Enzo Ducci, a local geologist with Gécamines who has done much useful work for us, on stretch of river from source to Kolwezi. Our Army Air Corps Beaver aircraft is still on its way to us from Britain. Therefore this morning I flew in small private aeroplane to examine river south of Kolwezi. My deputy, Mike Gambier, and our chief engineer (boats), Jim Masters accompanied me. A very bumpy ride, all sick. Discovered twenty-five kilometres of river blocked with trees and vegetation. Looked for suitable place to launch boats and found likely spot where river nears Zambian border by village of Mushima. Took Polaroid pictures of first falls, rapids and approach tracks. One slightly tricky fall within a few kilometres of our start point. Landed midday and discussed findings with our intelligence officer (IO), Peter Marett.

Expedition preparations continued throughout the day. Spent evening learning speech in French with my PA, Pam Baker. Arranged to borrow Victor Forrest's Islander aircraft for tomorrow to do air reconnaissance to north as far as the Gates of Hell. Morale high, everyone eager to get moving. Stores continued to arrive from Lubumbashi.

Monday 7 October

Flew in Islander to Kongolo. Paid particular attention to rapids immediately north of Kolwezi. The pre-expedition reconnaissance warned me that these very likely to be impassable. Saw two bad falls[1] in a gorge of reddish rock that will certainly require portage. Named area the Red Gorge. Using Polaroid and ordinary cameras recorded conditions from Kolwezi to Bukama. Many rapids and of course the dams themselves to contend with. Portage will again be necessary. Hope to confirm details by foot reconnaissance. Saw hippo, elephant and buck along river bank. No crocodiles. From Bukama overflew great swamp of Upemba and thence north to Kongolo. Navigation no problem on this stretch. Relatively little habitation.

At Kongolo saw the Gates of Hell. Water dangerously low and doubtful if navigation possible at this level. Local people assured me water will rise within the month. I wonder? Filmed this dauntingly named stretch of narrows and rapids. Certainly at high water it would be impassable. Must now hope to get just sufficient water for us to clear rocks without turning whole stretch into foaming tumbling mass.

[1]The worst of these was nicknamed Paddington Falls

No fuel for aircraft at Kongolo therefore forced to fly east towards Lake Tanganyika and landed at Kalemie (formerly Albertville). Lake Tanganyika like a vast inland sea, azure blue with long palm-fringed golden beaches. Pilot calculated insufficient daylight for return to Kolwezi therefore forced to stay night. Lieutenant Bongo (LO) arranged accommodation at Hôtel du Lac. Town very quiet and tense. Local terrorist problems. Armed troops much in evidence.

Tuesday 8 October

Awoke to find streets outside hotel lined with armed soldiers. As sun rose over lake troops moved off in vehicles on an operation. Atmosphere still tense. People regard us with suspicion, although we are unarmed. It is fortunate we have an LO with us. Another useful asset is our special expedition arm badge which carries the MPR [Mouvement Populaire de la Révolution] flag and therefore indicates that we are at least on the side of President Mobutu.

Flew back to Kolwezi across rising hills and savannah parkland. Magnificent waterfalls and rapid strewn rivers, all tributaries of the Zaire. Small herds of game seen on the plain. Re-examined area of the Red Gorge and decided to deploy a bank reconnaissance group. Main lesson learnt from this air reconnaissance is the vast distance involved in this enormous country and the logistic problems of this expedition have now been highlighted. I conclude that wherever possible I must move by water and therefore it will be necessary to increase size of the fleet that I propose to assemble at Bukama. The river is the key to movement.

On landing found my right eardrum had burst, undoubtedly due to rapid descent with a mild head cold. Some discomfort, wretched nuisance especially at such a busy time. Evening dinner with Lions Club of Kolwezi. People, both black and white, very friendly and most hospitable.

Wednesday 9 October

The overwhelming hospitality from local people continues. One or two members rather over-indulged and had to be brought to heel. Held final O (orders) group for whole expedition this morning and moved off to river at 1115 hours. Six hours travel through dense bush on good track to point where engineer section under Major Ernie Durey had cut path to river. Gambier Force, as I have named the initial party, moving with boats. My Tac HQ is to accompany for first three days. Reached river and launching site late afternoon. Captain Nigel Warren of the Gurkhas acted as pathfinder and with his forward support team (FST) assisted us in making camp. Surprisingly no game seen.

Heavy rain fell at 1700 hours. First we have seen. Usual commotion of people settling in to an expedition; i.e. losing common items of equipment. Message from base to say Beaver aircraft left Britian 6 October.

Examined river late in day and found it approximately fifteen to twenty metres wide, fringed by tall palms and jungle. Away from river there is typical bush country. Village of Mushima reportedly nearby. No natives seen.

Thursday 10 October

A fine day with no rain.

Distance covered: 13 km. Start point: $11°37.7'S$, $25°52.8'E$. End point: $11°21'S$, $25°43.4'E$.

Terrain: two small falls in first four kilometres in area $11°36.6'S$, $25°53'E$, then long easy stretches interspersed with shallows. Except in rapids current less than 2 km per hour. Rapids proved no great problem and were easily navigated by boat.

Vegetation: forest verging to mushito along the river edge, then normal savannah.

Zoology: two hippo seen, one an enormous adult. An antelope and abundance of birds also seen. They included kingfishers, weavers, herons, darters, ground hornbills, bee-eaters and kites. At night crocodile count revealed two crocodile and one hippo in two kilometres.

Habitation: one small village, believed to be Lualenga. A bark canoe and fish trap seen; the canoe is the first I have noted of this type.

Entomology: mosquitoes were absent, although occasional tsetse and horsefly seen.

No radio contact established. Night bitterly cold, 13°C.

Friday 11 October

Distance covered: 36·5 km. End point: 11°10·8'S, 25°37'E. Altitude: 1325 metres.

Navigation: easy stretches of river up to fifty metres wide with a few rocky shallows; no particular hazards.

Vegetation: mushito and dambo opening out some five kilometres from start point to savannah forest.

Geology: rocks reported to be pre-cambrian sediment only.

Water sampling: Major Roger Chapman, Green Howards is collecting samples every twenty kilometres.

Zoology: a small herd of four to five hippo seen. Three crocodiles and one small antelope seen. Bird life continues as yesterday plus one ibis and glossy starlings, also marabou storks and duck. Storks in great abundance on two large trees.

Medical: no problems yet, few mosquitoes.

Habitation: two villages in which Swahili and Kisanga were spoken. Some canoes and fish traps plus nets and fishing lines in evidence. People very friendly.

General observation: accuracy of the 1:200000 scale map generally good. Radio frequency is over-subscribed and thus communication difficult; propose to change time of radio schedule. Morale good and weather warm. One light shower during the day. Boats suffering minor problems with engines and slight leaks.

Saturday 12 October

Distance covered: 22·2 km. End point: 11°06·2'S, 25° 31·8'E. Altitude: 1310 metres.

Navigation: long easy stretches followed by island complex and numerous waterfalls over a distance of two kilometres. Between rapids, the boats with 20 hp engines tow those with 4½ hp. This speeds progress and saves fuel.

Vegetation: mushito, dambo and savannah plain.

Geology: the pre-cambrian sediment continues, plus some quartz. Geomorphological sampling continues every two kilometres.

Zoology: no game seen. No unusual birds. Five fish (carp) purchased from local fishermen.

Habitation: two small villages with fish traps and nets. People friendly. A warm, sunny day with some rain at night.

Boats received damage from a two-kilometre tangle of rapids, tree-stumps and rocky outcrops. Crews tired but happy. I noted that after their initial reticence, boats' parties now wash daily in the river.

Election results in Britain reached us by radio.

Sunday 13 October

Distance covered: 18 km. End point: 11°03·2'S, 25°33·5'E. Altitude: 1295 metres.

Terrain: no change, except that more islands appearing in the river which is gradually getting wider. The banks have a more tropical appearance as we move north.

Zoology: zoologist Dr Alan Bartram put out fish net tonight. Less animal and bird life seen today.

Entomology: less flies and insects but day colder and overcast.

Habitation: three canoes seen. People obviously depend on the river for livelihood. Much evidence of fishing.

General administrative points: more lemonade powder is required in the rations.

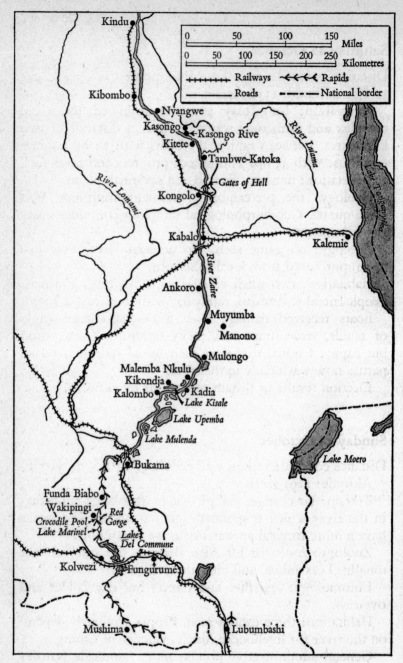

Source to Kindu

A generally cloudy day although sunny early with showers in the afternoon. The chaplain held Sunday service in the field this afternoon. Had hoped to find FST/B waiting for us. But not found at rendezvous. Tac HQ left river and returned overland to base. Mike Gambier continued in command of fleet. Fleet now only nineteen kilometres from Kolwezi road bridge. At night the fleet had reached FST/B in the nick of time as fuel was exhausted and rations low. Hippo disturbed boat parties during night. Tac HQ at base. Botanists and entomologists deployed at Fungurume examining copper solution pollution and collecting insects. Sergeant-Major Eddie McGee, APTC, requires more support for his group and I have sent Maggie Bush, one of our girl secretaries, to join him. Met close recce section (CRS) at Kolwezi Bridge, their morale high. Lieutenant Dick Festorazzi, RE, went back with fuel for them. A puncture caused problems due to the lack of a wheel brace, which warns me that greater care must be taken in preparation of vehicles. On return Dick found hit-and-run victim in road. Situation could have been difficult but fortunately there were some witnesses. Captain Kayalo (Senior LO) sorted it out. Valerie Jones came in from FST/A to work with support group.

Preparations continuing for advance north. Ground recce in progress. Local people, both black and white, believe we are mercenaries. Every attempt being made to convince them that we are simply a scientific expedition.

Monday 14 October

Distance covered by fleet: 18 km. Camped on bend of river directly south of Kolwezi Lake. Night temperature: 58°F (max). Midday: 110°F.

Terrain: more islands and palm trees. River rocky, navigation more difficult.

Geology: as before, but with limestone outcrops now appearing.

Zoology: six fish caught in overnight net included carp and mormyrid. Otherwise main interest was a hippo that wandered into the camp, made a bit of noise and ran around for a while before returning to the water. Another large one seen in river. Natives do not appear to hunt or trap them. Crocodile strangely absent, only one seen today. Fish eagles common.

Habitation: six bark canoes and six dug-outs seen; also two very large fish traps. Workmanship poor.

Tuesday 15 October

Gambier force at Kolwezi Bridge 1300 hours. Grand reception provided by Simba Breweries. Commissaire du Zone and local dignitaries present. Beer in great abundance and transport kindly provided by the Forrests. Captain Richard Skaife, our signals officer, used the Sony videotape equipment for the first time. Most impressed with its performance and consider it will be of greatest value to us in months ahead. Simplicity of machine is wonderful and results very good. Everyone in high spirits and whole exercise was good for public relations!

Wednesday 16 October

We hear today that the Beaver is in Lagos and has gone unserviceable with compass trouble. All fuel very short and Derek Jackson will visit Kinshasa to obtain permission from Presidency on many matters, including the hire of a train for his logistic group and permission to buy fuel from government sources. Even with maximum economy we cannot move without a certain amount of petrol. The real problem will come when our aircraft arrives.

I am worried about the possibilities of any drunkenness among our men in the bars of Kolwezi.

Evening party to entertain our Zaire LOs went very well. Ground recce parties still out in area of Red Gorge. Meanwhile Captain Tom Mabe, US Army, and our US white-water expert Marc Smith are preparing giant craft. The Johnson engines apparently sent from Belgium have failed to arrive and this could cause a problem as we only have seven other 40 hp outboard motors and I need a minimum of nine for safety.

Thursday 17 October

All recce parties in from Red Gorge area. Conference held in morning and decided on three-kilometre portage. Usual hawks and doves conflict, just as on Blue Nile. However, I left no room for argument. At this stage of the game it would be foolhardy to risk men's lives unnecessarily in suicidal attempt to cross waterfalls. Our aim is not to attempt to keep boats on the river all the way, but to carry out a scientific exploration.

Money very tight so we are trying to raise funds locally by showing films of previous expeditions in the town. Have collected 170 zaires so far. (One zaire is worth approximately £1.) Radio discipline still not good and office needs tightening up. I feel my Tac HQ cannot move out until these things are sorted out. There is a need for a general overall coordination of adminstration. Nevertheless the achievements of our support group are remarkable.

Issued confirmatory notes for Operation Bullfrog, the name I have given to the next phase which will get the fleet to Bukama. One or two group commanders taking an independent line had to be pulled up today. Problem largely due to our stretched communications. Still worried about possibilities of any clash with Zairois in Kolwezi bars.

Friday 18 October

Deployment to Bullfrog.[1] Hawks and doves simmer as regards crossing of falls in Red Gorge. Much of this I put

[1] To save time Gambier Force was organized in two parties of two boats each.

B

down to generation gap! However, when they have seen the water the young bloods will eat their words. Final brief to Tom Mabe on move to Bukama overland, which he is to command.

Consider it possible Gambier Force will not reach Bukama by 25 October, but launching ceremony of giant craft must continue on that day as local dignitaries have been invited. Tac HQ moved out by Land-Rover and established itself in hospital at Le Marinel. Peter Marett had done excellent work and the briefing for the operation has turned out to be first class. Signals communications still weak. However, had long conversation with Derek Jackson in Kinshasa where he is pulling off the usual miracle. He is attempting to plan a logistic exercise with Zaire Army, using their giant Puma helicopters on the final phase of the expedition next January. The missing Johnson outboards have been found. Thank goodness.

The LOs are noticeably more suspicious of us and one or two are openly prickly. I have therefore had a confidential word with all group leaders, reference behaviour and the need for good public relations. Visited boats late evening, all in good heart having crossed over the Marinel dam. Thunderstorm with five-millimetre hailstones hit us in evening.

For this phase we are using Avon Professionals, fitted with oars as in earlier phase. There is some really ferocious white water here and it will certainly test the crews tomorrow. Scenery in these hills very pleasant and temperature not too hot. Operation proving quite enjoyable. Tac HQ base situated in hospital surrounded by garden of fantastic flame trees. Only one matter perturbed me tonight and that was the sudden appearance of a number of Angolans whom I suspect to be rebel soldiers having come here for medical treatment. They were in military uniform and looked very surprised to see us, whom they rightly assumed to be members of a foreign army. The Zaire LOs also seem worried about their presence and we kept firmly apart to avoid any confrontation.

Saturday 19 October

Mike Gambier and Lieutenant John Watkin, RM, both moved off from their bank positions at 0800 hours. Very easy journey, I am told, through moderate rapids. Nevertheless the water between dams was exciting and a trifle dangerous. Thanks to the water level being raised in the river by co-operative engineers at the dam site Gambier and Watkins reached Crocodile Pool at 1400 hours. They reported that there had been a moment of excitement when Ernie Durey and his sappers had jacked up a fallen wire footbridge about a metre above the water to allow boats to pass beneath. Near disaster struck as boats approaching at high speed when bridge supports broke and wire came snapping back down to water-level. Local people delighted with engineers' work; they now have a bridge again.

Masters' and Chapman's boats had a more exciting and hair-raising journey through numerous severe rapids and reached the end of their sector at 1800 hours. As last part of journey was over lake, they were towed in.

During day I recced the Red Gorge and was able to reaffirm our decision to portage at this point. It would be suicidal to attempt the waterfalls. Sides of gorge almost vertical. It is a chasm with a waterfall at both ends. Wild life seen on the edges of the gorge included oribi and other small antelopes. Baboons and monitor lizard also seen.

Visited FST/B camp at Crocodile Pool. Well organized by Nigel Warren and his Gurkhas. I entertained Chief Waki-pindgi to lunch. Introduced all members to him including Pam Baker whom he greeted with '*Bonjour, monsieur*'. Her pride was saved when we discovered that the old chief is almost blind! Pam is getting used to strange remarks. Recently when she met our Fijian corporal signaller, Sam Qarau, he said to her, 'Baker? That's interesting, my grandfather ate a missionary named Baker.'

Two very heavy rainstorms accompanied by thunder and lightning in the late evening. Heard on radio that our amphibious buggy had arrived at Kolwezi.

Sunday 20 October

Operation Bullfrog successfully completed. Both boat teams reunited at Crocodile Pool at 0930 hours. Held discussion on modification of Avon Professionals before leaving them and returning to base at Kolwezi.

Crews were in good heart, although strangely we are noticing the drop in temperature at night. Last night's minimum was 14°C. Left crews modifying boats and holding church service. They later sailed at 2130 hours. Mike Gambier, now in command of fleet, reported by radio that water conditions were initially rough but then settled and let the boats make good progress. Crews were now more expert at using a combination of engines and oars in turbulent waters, but at 1500 hours Gambier's own boat was swept sideways over a five-foot waterfall and nearly capsized. Camp had been made in area infested by blue-black centipedes and ants. The fleet had covered distance of twenty kilometres. Radio communications poor.

On return to base noticed a splendid old steam-roller that had been made in Britain and was now rusting in the bush. One wonders what stories it could tell. Today the main body of our force moved by rail to Bukama. Derek Jackson has not returned from Kinshasa. I visited FST/C at lake near Kolwezi.

Monday 21 October

Gambier Force moving on. They reported sailing at 0740 hours and maintaining an average speed of 10 km per hour. The Chaplain's hands were very swollen from insect bites of previous night.

Fleet had passed Funda Biabo with its old ferry at 1100 hours. At 1130 hours they were surprised by an innocent-looking band of rock which turned into a rapid and a four-foot waterfall. For half an hour the crews careered through a zigzag rock gorge hardly wide enough in which to row. Out of this and into another series of rapids with a six-foot waterfall. They portaged the obstruction and found a third series of zigzag rapids down which water was cascading very fast. The rocks are of hydrated conglomerates, which Ken McKechnie, one of our geologists, said should not be there! At 1525 hours they met FST/B who had luckily arrived one day ahead of schedule. Progress more rapid than expected, they consider fleet should reach Bukama in two and a half days. Gambier spent night with the FST whose efficiency and hard work he praised.

At base, Q (logistical) planning continued. The Beaver is expected any day.

Tuesday 22 October

Derek Jackson back after successful visit to Kinshasa. Throughout day we prepared for move forward. Resupply of Gambier Force went as planned. Communications still a worry, and as we become more stretched I fear that they will get worse. One of the problems is the difficulty in sending out the press releases to *The Daily Telegraph*. I have warned their correspondent that the maximum we can manage at the moment is three releases of approximately two hundred words each per week.

Gambier Force had late start at 0920 hours to allow letters and personal mail to be sent out with FST. All motors reported to be functioning well. At 1010 hours the TV camera team spent some time attempting to film a rather shy hippo. Not terribly successful but at lunchtime a family of three hippo had swum up and down for an hour for the camera's benefit!

At base my HQ kindly gave me a birthday party this evening and we also made our various farewells to all the people who have been so good to us at Kolwezi.

Wednesday 23 October

Major diplomatic problems today. Our LOs seemed to suspect that we are up to no good! I trust that our embassy in Kinshasa will be able to sort things out. Gambier reported sailing at 0730 hours across some very shallow patches interspersed with rapids. The river was again running through rocky gorges some twelve metres wide and the speed at this section was timed at approximately fourteen kilometres per hour. Fifty kilometres from Bukama they had seen a two-year-old elephant. Apparently these creatures are doing much damage to local crops. Baboons, barking like dogs, and flying fish were also reported.

Tac HQ moved by train during night to Bukama. During late afternoon Beaver arrived at last. They had an epic flight out involving several near arrests but were in good heart and we were very glad to see them.

Thursday 24 October

Arrived Bukama early to be met by local officials and Captain Tom Mabe. Hospitality excellent and I consulted LOs with regard to our diplomatic problems.

Gambier Force said to be twenty-three kilometres up river from town, making slow progress in difficult rapids. They report that local chief had given them traditional gift for travellers; in this case a chicken! Later Mike Gambier's own boat was attacked and nearly sunk by a large hippo.

Apparently it was a pretty frightening moment, but repairs were effected and the crippled craft taken in tow. Progress was considerably slowed down as the engines were beginning to develop trouble.

The amphibious buggy driven by Captain Paul Turner was extremely useful in Bukama and is used to run about between our temporary base and the riverside where boats are being assembled.

Already a team of scientists consisting of entomologists and botanists in small craft has advanced into the swamp to the north. They are being looked after by Sergeant-Major McGee. We shall pick them up when we move forward with the main fleet. They have sent warning of weed some 150 kilometres ahead.

Friday 25 October

Gambier Force reported still twenty-three kilometres away struggling in bad rapids. They may reach here today. One private aircraft arrived from Lubumbashi with Mr and Mrs Harold Shakespear of Barclays International together with the United States and Belgian Consuls. Later our Beaver arrived from Kolwezi with the Commissaire du Sous-Région.

President Mobutu is in Lubumbashi after attending the independence celebrations in Lusaka. Therefore some officials we invited were unable to come. Nevertheless launching ceremony of *Barclays Bank*, one of the giant inflatables, was very successful and went off at 1530 hours. Tom Mabe did excellent job in organizing events. Sappers had dug ramp through river bank, and the boat was launched with much speech-making and a splash of champagne. Thousands of people watched and joined in fun cheering wildly as the boat moved a token distance downstream. Paul Turner fell in river whilst trying his hand at paddling a canoe, causing much mirth!

At nightfall word came that two boats of Gambier Force had been badly damaged. We heard more details of the hippo attack and also that one boat had been damaged on rocks. Ernie Durey and his sappers immediately sallied forth to recover the party. Two boats did in fact reach the town late this evening. Meanwhile local people laid on great party which we attended. Party continued until early hours. One of our Gurkhas has been taken ill and Pam Baker is nursing him. Dr Edouard Vinke, the anthropologist from Lubumbashi, has joined us. Dr Enzo Ducci also arrived to see us briefly. He plans to join the fleet at Kisangani (formerly Stanleyville).

Two Belgians who had hoped to join the expedition arrived, but they were clearly unacceptable to our LOs and so we had to refuse them. They kindly left with us a stock of food that they had intended to use on the expedition.

Saturday 26 October

Spent day bringing in Gambier Force. They had very lucky escape when hippo attacked. One boat was completely destroyed and lost. Also heard that two very expensive television cameras and much equipment was lost in a rapid when boat overturned. Gambier told story of an epic few days. Apparently on 25 October they had found that shooting rapids under tow is impossible, and hence the tow must be slipped before the white water and taken again below the dangerous stretch. They had negotiated a narrow cleft some five kilometres long in a band of volcanic rock, preceded by an S-bend, complicated by a large boulder in the middle, on to which Jim Master's boat was driven and holed in four places. Emergency repairs barely staunched the flow and the crew were forced to bale continuously.

The fleet was now left with two good and two crippled craft with only one sound engine and a second funtioning on only a single cylinder. But their troubles were just starting. By mid-morning the boats had entered a fast flowing S-bend, twelve metres wide, three hundred metres long, preceded by a four-foot waterfall. Roger Chapman's boat capsized and Hugh Davies of The Daily Telegraph was almost drowned. This was when most of the camera and sound equipment had been lost.

Two hours' reconnaissance down both sides of the river revealed that the way was blocked by large waterfalls and narrow rocky clefts, quite unsuitable for the fleet. The boats were therefore lined with ropes to a more suitable place and a camp was made below the village of Kalenge. Since they were only twelve kilometres from Bukama it was decided to portage the two good boats round to a launching site below the rock barrier and for the remainder of the force to march out to the road on the next day. So when the crews eventually reached us in the evening they were pretty exhausted. The Beaver had done some excellent work in trying to link up the parties and act as a radio relay. The hippo-crippled Professional was buried over the falls. Quite an exciting time.

At Bukama we have been undergoing major reorganization of the expedition. One or two minor personality problems caused by the terrifying experiences in the white water to the south. In view of the complicated and vital problems of supply to the fleet, I have appointed Major Roger Champman as overall quartermaster to fleet and, Tom Mabe will therefore become skipper of *Barclays Bank*.

Dr Vinke made good finds of tenth-century pottery, skulls, spear and arrowheads in river bank here today.

Evacuated sick Gurkha by air, sending Pam Baker with him. Looks like chicken-pox! Generally, spirits good all round. Local officials returned in various aircraft.

Sunday 27 October

Beaver arrived for recce at 0730 hours, bringing with it news from Derek Jackson. This included a report on our political problems and details of logistic difficulties. Communications continue to be difficult and we must make every effort to improve them, for as we advance it will be vital to maintain contact. Fleet sailed at midday and made thirty-one kilometres.

Night location: 9°05·2'S, 26°00·2'E in great Upemba swamp.

Terrain: mild swamp, fairly dry.

Navigation: no problems, river up to 300 m wide. Current: 4–5 km per hour. Water low.

Vegetation: lush and an unknown species collected for Kew.

Geology: conglomerate near Bukama, then alluvial plain.

Entomology: comparatively little. Ants numerous.

Anthropology: Tshiluba is spoken. A few fishing villages with fields of maize and manioc. The area obviously one where the people suffer from sickle cell anaemia.

Medical: general health of members good.

Zoology: snowy egrets, boo-boo-shrikes, herons and large herd of hippo seen in river.

Boats: the bolts on transom sheared through on *Barclays Bank*, otherwise performance good, but Johnson 20 hp engines giving trouble.

The first day's cruise with the giant boats has been a success, but at night we were subjected to the heaviest tropical storm yet experienced. Hippo[1] very numerous. Giant boats using four to five gallons each per day.

Monday 28 October

Distance covered: 42 km. Arrived at Mulenda. Location: 08°43·8′S, 26°03·7′E.

Navigation: easy, apart from hazard of hippo.

Vegetation: entering papyrus swamp.

Terrain: marsh with peripheral hills to the east.

Vegetation: mango plentiful, also maize, banana and manioc.

Entomology: few butterflies and moths, possibly because of rainy season. Many mosquitoes. One large predatory water-bug and one lantern fly seen.

Anthropology: many layers of pottery found along river bank. Red clay pottery collected.

Medical: much measles and gastro-enteritis found in villages. No onchocerciasis (oncho).

Zoology: reports of elephant and bush-buck spoor, hippo numerous. Shining blue kingfishers seen, also fish eagles and open-billed storks. Darter birds quite common. One

[1] One threatened me in night; chased off with loudhailer.

snake seen swimming in river and two great snowy pelicans seen at Mulenda village, probably brought in from Lake Mulenda a couple of years ago.

Boats: fuel consumption increased to 7–8 gallons per day for the giant craft, caused by the additional distance run. Johnsons continue to give trouble and are drinking petrol! Discussed boat performance with Marc Smith and decided we could open up the throttles slightly more on the new 40 hp Mercury engines.

All indications are that it is impossible to obtain fuel. Therefore we must exercise maximum economy on voyage north. After dark we crossed river to visit chief. He offered us palm wine but then couldn't find any! Local sick treated by our doctor. We have now met up with entomologists and botanists who will be continuing north with the fleet.

Tuesday 29 and Wednesday 30 October

Early-morning palm-wine ceremony when chief arrived with bottles from village. Custom demanded I take a sip of this extremely alcholic beverage. Did so with no ill effects although others who indulged suffered badly later! Decided we should sail through the night to save time as scientists not especially interested in the stretch immediately ahead. To save petrol took aboard logs with which to make fires for cooking.

Distance run during daylight: 55 km, distance run during night: 38 km, total 93 km. Fleet arrived at Kalombo 2235 hours on 29 October. Location: 8°18·1'S, 26°19·2'E.

Terrain: typical swamps.

Navigation: river beginning to break up into many islands.

Entomology: rich in insects.

Anthropology: found sites rich in pottery from fifth to ninth century, reports of at least two skeleton sites.

Medical: general health on expedition continues good. Eye surgeon Dr John Chapman-Smith saw approximately thirty patients in Kalombo. Some children were quite sick with a wide variety of illnesses.

Zoology: heavy storm in Upemba lake has caused death of many fish. Probably due to deoxidization of water when stirred up. Mormyrids and cichlid population in Lake Kisale collected. Olive baboon and hippo seen. Many purple herons and open-billed storks. Fish eagle and black-shouldered kite seen. Acides flies' eggs found and shipped to base.

Vegetation: papyrus studied in three lakes, growth pattern and performance differs greatly in these three sites. There is unique pattern of metabolism of photosynthesis found in the eight types of grasses in the swamps.

Local Catholic mission school visited the fleet in afternoon and spent an hour looking at our boats. We briefed them on the expedition and told them that the Scientific Exploration Society sent parties to carry out similar work all over the world.

People very friendly and we had a soccer match with them. Their team, the local champions and named the Serpents, won easily; good time had by all. In the evening attended dancing arranged in town in our honour. Mail, very welcome, had arrived by Beaver. Also urgently needed supply of biscuits.

Cash and fuel situation is growing worse and causing me real concern. Sent small party to visit chief of Kikondja during day to try to get fuel. They had no success but returned with beer. Chief was apparently most congenial. Continued sailing through the vast marsh and on through night. Heavy rain is frequent at night and the storms are quite dramatic. Fantastic thunder and lightning. Hippo still numerous in river and on banks.

Thursday 31 October

Distance travelled: 141 km.

Fleet moved into Lake Kisale where we washed and

swam. Lake found to be only 1½ m deep. Had intended to spend twenty-four hours near Kikondja and sent recce group ahead to find suitable camp site. Kikondja is a well-planned and neatly laid-out town of 57 000 inhabitants, but because it is surrounded by much agriculture we were unable to find good camp site. Took beer with chief of Kikondja and as he told me that the area was extremely unhealthy I decided to sail on to Mulongo.

Bird life across the lake fascinating, amazing variety. Fishing pirogues dotted the water as far as the eye could see and fishing nets made navigation difficult. Water also very shallow. Every available piece of dry land had a fisherman's hut. Papyrus grows everywhere as well as various types of weed and lilies. River channel difficult to find since most of original navigation marks rotted away. Channel is roughly marked by tree-stumps. As daylight faded we stopped at the small village of Kadia on edge of this great treeless swamp for our evening meal. The night was beautiful, moonlit and slightly misty, but thankfully with no navigational hazards. Tom Mabe gave Ernie Durey's sappers a tow and found himself with thirty-one people on board!

Friday 1 November

Arrived Mulongo at 0700 hours after long night cruise through marsh land with a few navigational problems mainly caused by islands of papyrus. One of these had to be dynamited by the engineers. Terrain was narrow alluvial plain with pre-cambrian hills surrounding it. Our entomologists collected many butterflies and the anthropologist made a number of contacts but did no collecting. The medical officer found that measles was a great problem amongst local people but our only illness seemed to be dysentery. Many bats seen and our fish team continued to collect very satisfactorily. A rare bird, the black-winged stilt, was seen. This is fairly unusual in Central Africa.

On arrival at Mulongo we met FST/A. They were in good heart although Corporal Newell was in a missionary hospital through having drunk some untreated water. I have tightened up water discipline considerably as the river is now known to contain bilharzia, hook-worm and possibly leptospirosis. There was one mildly amusing incident which involved one of our scientists allegedly striking a Zaire LO. Although it sounded serious at first it transpired to be a case of the scientist protecting some rare specimen which the LO was in the act of manhandling! With the help of Lieutenant Bongo the matter was sorted out to everyone's satisfaction.

Have noticed that the FST Land-Rovers are over-laden but with transport so short and no more money to hire vehicles we can do nothing about this at the moment.

In Mulongo we met two charming missionaries, Mary Goodsell, who was from Britain and has been here for forty-four years and Dolly MacDonald from Australia who has been here twenty-eight years. Together they ran the Protestant mission and were extremely hospitable to us. We lunched with them and had baths in their house.

At evening O Group I gave members a general rocket for selfishness and pointed out that many are putting themselves before the needs of the team.

We are gradually beginning to look more like a travelling zoo. Pam Baker has acquired a rather attractive thick-tailed bush-baby, which is much admired, and other pets include scientist Peter Hudson's fish eagle, named Compo, several chickens and a chameleon.

I hear there is fuel at Manono thanks to the efforts of Lieutenant Somue (LO) and Pam. They went ahead the other night and made contact with a chief who, after receiving some medical attention from Pam, promised to have fuel available in advance of us. Therefore am sending FST/A on ahead to purchase £120 worth. One or two scientists have joined the fleet from the FST who of course came up from the Upemba area. Among these are the Haselwoods and Marie-Thérèse Guichard, one of our nurses.

There is a lot of carelessness with equipment; it is being left about and I have had to reprimand quartermasters most firmly tonight. People cannot seem to realize that once we have lost something there is no means of replacing it.

Saturday 2 and Sunday 3 November

The fleet advanced once more with the Royal Engineers' raft being deployed to Muyumba to ferry the two Land-Rovers of FST/A across the Zaire. The heavily laden vehicles were almost too much for the raft which sat very low in the water, but the engineers did a good job and everything went smoothly. John Benham-Crosswell was in good spirits. One of the M650 boats has gone missing during the move out and an Avon Professional has been used to replace it in the raft. The performance of this raft, which was the same one we used in Darien, is only slightly impaired as a result of this modification. After the rafting operation the close recce section went on to Ankoro. One craft broke down when the pull-start on the Mercury came away and could not be replaced. This is a general weakness which we have noticed before but we must carry tools to be able to repair this on the move.

Tac HQ travelled with the recce section and we all met with FST/A in Ankoro at 1900 hours, spending the night in a priory.

The main fleet arrived at 0540 hours and after an abortive attempt to find a good camp site we decided to use the warehouses at the water's edge. Ankoro is situated at the junction of various rivers and is a natural trading point. It is very run-down, however, and most of the main buildings are in ruins. The large hospital is without a doctor. An impressive cathedral stands on the hill above the little town but we saw no white people anywhere; a rather eerie place. One of the rivers at this point comes from Lake Tanganyika, which it drains. I sent the recce section on ahead but they failed to reach Kongolo. Meanwhile we hear that the train carrying our support groups has reached Kongolo and base camp is being set up.

We are now deploying a small scientific party to the north-west so that they may travel down the Lomami. They are to seek the rare pygmy chimpanzee and the group will be commanded by Lieutenant Bob Hudson, Royal Marines. It will take them approximately a month to go down the river and they should meet us in December at Kisangani.

The journey to Ankoro had covered a distance of 160 kilometres. The terrain was receding swamp, and steep mud banks were now appearing leading up into wooded savannah. Few flood plains were noticed. Water problems continued to plague the fleet and the engineers are now assisting in providing a regular supply of drinking water. Every Millbank bag (canvas filter bags) we have is in use.

During the voyage our craft have been very crowded and people have had to endure a certain amount of discomfort at night. One of the greatest problems has been the lack of any form of toilet facilities on board. While cruising at night it is not easy to find a suitable landing point so that people may go ashore and commune with nature. It is therefore normal for the stern of the boat to be set aside for that purpose! Usually this works well but last night one of our ladies had gone to the stern when we heard a shriek. Apparently she had squatted down almost on top of one of our Zaire LOs. The poor chap had a very nasty awakening! This is one of the problems with mixed races on board a boat, it is rather hard to see a black man on a dark night!

Entomology: a very good butterfly collection was made. Large, because it was made actually in a village. There were many flying ants and termites.

Vegetation: borassus palm seen. Tin mine was investigated and compared with the results at Fungurume. Much agricultural land here.

Zoology: a large number of species of fish here, especially catfish and in much greater quantities than before. All fish were caught by nets. Fairly alkaline river, relatively clean and with little silt. Little diversity in fish parasites. In the village we saw civets, baboon, porcupine and a kingfisher. Local people make pets of the animals and sell them. Many snakes. One found on beach in act of swallowing frog and it disappeared amongst our packs before it could be collected. Zoologist Dr Roger Sweeting has two black kites that are extremely tame. We are now seeing more long-crested hawk eagles, possible barbets? We have found earthworms for the first time since Bukama. Green monkeys were seen and the engineers saw some crocodile.

Anthropology and Archaeology: very important cemetery was found with various pottery pieces. During day a strange symbolic ceremony was held in town, the significance of which is unknown. Dancers with masks and ceremonial dress, plus skins of leopard and lion were in the streets. Some consternation was caused amongst the LOs about photographs being taken.

The close recce section plus Pam Baker and Marc Smith have gone ahead to the Gates of Hell. We shall stay here at least another day for scientific work.

Monday 4 November

Zoology: some interesting fish caught in the overnight net. Included polypterus. There is still a distinct lack of barbus. Several hollow-bill storks were seen across the river and strangely guinea pigs were found in the town. Assumed these to be escaped pets as they are not indigenous to this area. Black crakes and chameleons added to the zoological scene.

Entomology: large water-bugs. Very interesting collection of moths were gathered in the light traps last night; also long-horned grasshoppers.

Medical: doctors visited enormous but deserted hospital in town. Only two maternity cases there.

Anthropology: little native art about and only few simple school-children's carvings to be bought. Had one or two mix-ups over photographs and these had to be sorted out by the LOs.

We were able to collect a little clean water from the mission. This is a rare treat.

Tuesday 5 November

Jim Masters, Ernie Durey, Peter Marett, plus Captain Keba of the Zaire Navy and myself moved to Kongolo. We took with us Dr Vinke who is to return to Lubumbashi. The heavily laden M 650 would not go on the aquaplane so we were late into Kongolo after hitting sand-banks repeatedly. Arrived after dark. Town well organized by FST/C who had done a good job. Expedition is to be accommodated in ex-Belgian colonial houses which now stand deserted but are very habitable. Meanwhile fleet moved up behind us, and during night went badly aground on some sand-banks by Kabalo.

Derek Jackson is here with his special train. What a fantastic sight! A train in the middle of Africa, laden with rations, supplies, fuel, vehicle spares and a complete surgery.

Gordon Mitchell prowls up and down, the guardian of all we own. Meals are served in the railway siding. The expedition office is in a wagon-lit.

Wednesday 6 November

The day spent on administrative planning at Kongolo. Meanwhile reconnaissance of Gates of Hell continues. Water still low and there appears to be no great problem. Only difficulty is exposed rock. Recce is being done by ground, boat and air. The Sony video camera has been fitted in Beaver and is proving very useful, as are the Polaroid cameras.

Victor Forrest's Islander arrived bringing editor of *Mwanga*, whose correspondent Citoyen Mpoy is with us. Beaver is here but WO 1 Cliff Taylor has badly scalded himself with hot water and is looking quite a mess. He will not be fit to fly for many days yet. There is no doubt that the LOs are losing patience with one or two of our less considerate members and I have repeatedly to warn our people about their conduct. Noted that the train had red and green lights! How very appropriate for a river expedition.

Fleet arrived at 2030 hours.

Over radio we have heard that medical research team are now to be deployed to Kananga (formerly Luluabourg), taking with them some three Range Rovers supplied by the Zaire Government. That is 400 miles from where we expected them to work and will cause considerable logistic problems. I am sure that Freddie Rodger has good reason for this change of plan, and only hope we can give him proper support.

Thursday 7 November

Refitting and reorganizing. Captain Kayalo (the senior LO) turned up with fifty-three weapons! These included 9 mm, .22, .30, 12 bore, and signal pistols. Apparently these are to replace the ones we were not allowed to bring from Britain at the last moment. These weapons will be of little value for zoological collecting purposes, and I have my suspicions that we have been armed for another reason. There are rumours of terrorists in the forests to the north and east.

Chimp Force, as we call Bob Hudson's group, are moving down the Lomami River, having been dropped off by FST/A who themselves will now go on to Kindu. Expedition is moving on schedule, although fuel continues to be a problem and our heavily laden Land-Rovers will not last much longer on the bad roads.

This evening gave a small party for local dignitaries. Learned much about the original Kongolo massacre in 1962 when some twenty-two priests were slaughtered and eaten.

The long, rather dull journeys on this uneventful part of the river have caused some members to get bored and we have a number of minor personality problems to sort out as a result. Now with the first rapids coming up to test the boats, people are certainly looking more interested. I keep telling them that beyond Kinshasa lie the great rapids of the Livingstone Falls which will certainly be a test when the time comes. Meanwhile we must content ourselves with the less dramatic rapids that now lie ahead. However, these could certainly be a problem and would indeed be very difficult in extremely low or very high conditions. Reports reaching me about the rapids in the Stanley Falls area are perturbing and it may be that we shall have to portage there.

Friday 8 November

Reorganization continued and we issued the guns that had been brought down yesterday. Arguments continue with LOs over minor matters. The logistic train is a great success and Derek Jackson, Tom Hawkins and Gordon Mitchell (our quartermaster) are doing an excellent job. Communications are improving, thanks to our signals section's hard work. Sergeant Dave Hudson, one of our signallers, even managed to get through to Kinshasa from the train, whilst it was moving recently. Not bad over a thousand miles distance!

The slow movement that is forced on us by difficulties of resupply is still causing some unrest among our more adventurous members. Land-based people want to get on the boat and some of the boat crew want to get on the land. This is probably due to the lack of excitement on the boats in the last ten days. The scientists, however, seem very happy indeed with their tasks and the general medical state is good, thanks to John Chapman-Smith and Ian Young. Peter Knudsen, our Danish doctor, is also doing an excellent job with a local hospital. Political problems continue to occupy much of my time. Tom Hawkins will have to join his BAOR unit in December, but I feel that with his knowledge of French and the local people it would be wise if he stays. I therefore wrote to the committee in London to see if this might be arranged.

On the flank our scientists continue to deploy and are moving forward to Kindu. The fish team will continue with the fleet.

I am amazed how well our civilians are putting up with the discomfort and primitive living conditions that we soldiers tend to accept as part of expedition life. The scientists really are a charming and extremely patient group of people. A great stalwart in their ranks is Dorothy Bovey, our botanical illustrator, who cheerfully takes all in her stride. Andrew Paterson, an enthusiastic young botanist is another excellent person who is always prepared to devote time to explaining his work to the soldiers.

Saturday 9 November

Through the Gates of Hell. In fact our fish section went through by accident yesterday. They were extremely lucky to avoid serious injury when one of the inflatable boats from which they were working was suddenly drawn through the narrow entrance of the Gates and went down a formidable stretch of water. The fishing net had become tangled in the propeller which had stopped the engine at a crucial moment. However, all was well and safe. Fleet moved into rapids at 0900 hours and with the flagship *La Vision* leading, we inched our way forward to the lip of the first fall. Marc Smith was at the helm and did an expert job in taking us through. All boats followed without incident and we progressed steadily down the various cataracts and rapids of this dangerous area. As a reminder of the power of the river, a wrecked steamer sat on rocks some seven metres above the present water-level! We understand it was deposited there after dragging its anchor at the time of the floods. The stark black rocks stood out all around us but the water was not too powerful and, apart from one very narrow passage which we had to shoot with great care, we passed through Gates without incident.

Night location: 5°09·8'S, 26°59·8'E. Distance travelled: 30 km.

Navigation: rapids and stretches of narrow water between metamorphised rock reefs. First rapid considered Grade 2 and the final narrow chute a Grade 4 on the Smith scale. Our very thorough reconnaissance resulted in a relatively easy passage, but without such thorough preparation the going could have been extremely difficult and hazardous. I am sure Stanley could not have got through here with his boat, the *Lady Alice*.

Terrain: saw first signs of equatorial rain forest (semi-tropical), mostly secondary jungle. The rock was in part slate and there was a rift (possible basalt) for approximately two miles. Rock formation was so regular it had appearance of being man-made. On banks many epiphytes and lianas were seen.

Entomology: many insects at camp site including ants, prichoptera, and neuroptera.

Stanley's boat, Lady Alice. *Each of her five sections was eight feet long*

Zoology: the bird form is changing and we now see more African darters and waders. Monkeys and large antelope (possibly eland) seen, also two water snakes of a brown/green colour one metre long. One larger water snake was seen early in the day and tried to climb aboard the flagship. Two monitor lizards were spotted.

Medical: now definitely in oncho territory.

Boats: the transom was damaged on *Barclays Bank.*

In general morale good. There is some concern because Eric Rankin, one of our TV film team, came with the boats for part of the way and then left to return overland to base at Kongolo. He has not turned up and is lost. I told him to take guide from amongst local people and I wonder if in fact he did this. A search is being organized by the support group.

I now believe that we were issued with firearms more for self-protection than for zoological and scientific purposes. I have more information that there are still rebels in the forest to the north of Kongolo. I sincerely hope that our appearance of being a well-armed military force will deter them from any action against us. I have distributed weapons to guard against a surprise attack and briefed one or two people on emergency drill. It would clearly suit the rebels' aims to have publicity in the world press by attacking a large international expedition such as this. We would be a sitting target when trying to negotiate rapids. The Zaire Army is patrolling part of this area and we have seen flares after dark. Our LOs are uneasy and we are keeping a very careful watch.

Sunday 10 November

Night location: 4°46′S, 26°52·5′E. Distance travelled: 49 km. Tonight we camp at the place where Stanley must first have seen the river. From his writing I was able to identify the low ridge that runs to the east of the river. It was from here that he first viewed what was then known as the Lualaba, at its confluence with another river he called the Luama. The local chief soon arrived and after the usual exchange of pleasantries he pointed out that a large rock, which we could see through binoculars, was a monument to Stanley's first sighting of the river. The chief came with entourage in some fine canoes, rather larger than ones we have seen previously. They were very friendly and brought us small gifts of fruit for which we thanked them and gave tins of jam and other rations in return. No word or any sign of rebels.

The day's navigation has been varied, with some channels of fast water between the basalt rocks. In places the current was about eighteen kilometres per hour.

Terrain: rapids Grade 3 in places, savannah on banks.

Entomology: a great profusion of lace-wings and flying ants gathered about the lamps at night.

Zoology: hippo seen and fish nets laid at lunchtime at village called Kiyuza with good results. Three types of catfish, two types of caracins, a cichlid, a laeao and sardines were discovered, also an elephant snout fish. Unfortunately Pam's bush-baby, Tiddly-push, disappeared during the night. The local chief had told me that snakes abound in the area and I organized a hunt for some without success.

Vegetation: the main items of interest were echinocochlea, fragmytes and vossia.

Medical: a child was seen with glaucoma kiyuzu.

The boats were running well and we passed a broken-down ferry at the junction of the Shaba and Kivu provinces. This is the first such ferry we have seen. A further point of interest was that we noted bats catching moths on the surface of the water. We had used the moth as a bait for fishing.

In general a most interesting and rather historic day, for now we are really following in the steps of Stanley.

The Anglo-American expedition for the discovery of the Nile and Congo sources had set out from Bagamoyo on the east coast of Africa on 17 November 1874. Stanley's adventures and discoveries during the first two years of his journey across the continent had been considerable but in October 1876 he reached the great river which so tantalized him. On 16 October 1876 he skirted a range of hills to the east of the great river. Apparently the people were excessively timid and Stanley was extremely suspicious of the natives of that area. In his diary he states:

October 17th: Marched to Mkwanga, Uzura, West-north-west 12 miles.

After 4 miles march we came to where the Luama conflowed with the mighty river Lualawa, Lualaba or Ugarowa. Islands were seen in it. Across river was a low valley, open country unmarked with any peculiar eminence or elevation except Kijima 2000 feet above the valley. After reaching the end of the range which bounded the Luama Valley on the north, we turned north-westerly and entered Uzura. Whence we followed the course of the Lualaba as far as Lulindi River. At Mkwanga we met two Wangwana from Kasonga who gave us the news of the late massacre of an entire caravan on the road to Kasesa by Manyema treachery, and of the departure of Tippu-Tib – Hamed Hamudi – to avenge the massacre.

The next day Stanley marched a further eighteen miles north by west. He drove his men hard and crossed the wide and little populated plain beyond which he met the in-famous Tippu-Tib whom he described as a fine handsome

dark man of Arab extraction in the prime of life, who next
to Sayid Bin Habib was reckoned to be the first of the Arab
explorers. In his book, *Through the Dark Continent* (1878),
Stanley described the deal that he made with the Arab
slaver.

When we were alone, Tippu-Tib informed me that he had been
consulting with his friends and relatives, and they were opposed
to his adventuring upon such a terrible journey; but that, as he
did not wish to see me disappointed in my prospects, he had
resolved to accompany me a distance of sixty camps, each camp
to be four hours' march from the other, for the sum of 5000
dollars, on the following conditions:

1. That the journey should commence from Nyangwé in any
direction I choose, and on any day I mentioned.

2. That the journey should not occupy more time than three
months from the first day it was commenced.

3. That the rate of travel should be two marches to one halt.

4. That if he accompanied me sixty marches – each march of
four hours' duration – I should at the end of that distance return
with him back again to Nyangwé for mutual protection and
support, unless we met traders from the west coast, whom I
might accompany to the western sea, provided I permitted two-
thirds of my force to remain with him at Nyangwé.

5. That, exclusive of the 5000 dollars, I should provision 140
men during their absence from Mwana Mamba – going and
returning.

6. That if, after experience of the countries and the natives, I
found it was impracticable to continue the journey, and decided
upon returning before the sixty marches were completed, I should
not hold him responsible, but pay him the sum of 5000 dollars
without any deduction.

These terms I thought reasonable – all except article 4; but
though I endeavoured to modify the article, in order to ensure
full liberty to continue the journey alone if I thought fit, Tippu-
Tib said he would not undertake the journey alone, from a
distance of sixty camps to Mwana Mamba, even though 50,000
dollars were promised him, because he was assured he would
never return to enjoy the money. He would much prefer continuing with me down to the sea, for a couple of thousand

dollars more, to returning alone with his 140 men for 50,000 dollars. He agreed, however, after a little remonstrance, to permit the addition of article 7, which was to the effect that if he, Tippu-Tib, abandoned the journey through faint-heartedness, before the full complement of the marches had been completed, he was to forfeit the whole sum of 5000 dollars, and the return escort.

Having struck his bargain Stanley marches north-west on 23 October 1876, with his strong Arab escort.

Monday 11 November

I doubt if the scene has changed much since Stanley was here in 1876 and this morning we were entertained by a fine display of boatmanship from the local people who paddled their long canoes in unison around the river in front of us, much as they must have done a hundred years ago with more hostile intent.

Night location: Kasongo Rive. A rapidly deteriorating mosquito-ridden town that has long given way to the main centre of Kasongo which is some little distance inland and, being higher, is freer of mosquitoes. Total distance travelled today: 50 km. Tac HQ went ashore and visited FST/B and FST/C.

Zoology: gill nets were laid overnight and caught cat-fish, mormyrid, schilbe labeo and alestes. An interesting catch, also including interesting diogenes parasites. One gill net was deployed at lunchtime near the rapids, also with a good result, but absence of cichlids noted and also fewer parasites. Two snakes captured, one at the rapids, and one at Kasongo (one viper, one yellow and black banded snake), hippo and one eleven-foot crocodile seen by the recce group. Absence of mosquitoes on river noted.

Terrain: savannah.

Entomology: one large door beetle collected with a wing-span of 13 cm. Many lace-wings and flying ants plus a few scarab beetles.

The boats used ten gallons each during the run. We

managed to refuel from the FST at Kasongo but fuel is still a serious problem and in very short supply. Where we can buy it, it has now reached the equivalent of £2.50 per gallon! The navigation throughout the day has not been too difficult, a few shallows and one set of rapids at Kitate.

Fantastic reception from villagers all along the river who cheered and waved wildly as we went past. A broken ferry seen at Tambwe-Katoka. The river is broadening out and is approximately five hundred metres wide. We arrived at Kasongo Rive at 1500 hours. Heavy rain fell during the night and roads are described as being terrible. Radios have been giving trouble, especially small VHF sets. Both the A 40 and handy-talkies are constantly breaking down. The best sets we have are the National Panasonic type.

Tuesday 12 November

It took Stanley some three days to reach here (Kasongo) with his caravan from the point we left yesterday, which shows how much faster it is to move along the river. However, at this time he had only the *Lady Alice* with him. Until he had managed to hire more canoes he could not move his vast party by river.

The Beaver landed with technicians who attempted to repair our echo sounder which, alas, has given up. This is a great loss as without it I cannot take accurate soundings of the river easily. The technicians were not successful, and although the equipment will be back-loaded to base I fear it is beyond repair. I also learned details of Eric Rankin's adventure. Apparently he was dropped off by mistake on an island. Not even the boat crews realized it was such nor did Eric. As the boats sailed away he found he was unable to get off the island, and it was only through the help of friendly fishermen that eventually he reached the mainland where he was found next day.

The people here are extremely friendly and the local dancers gave a short performance for us. Because of the trouble with the VHF radios I have replaced them all by National Panasonic sets. Good communications are vital on this river.

The local people say that the river is full of bilharzia and also crocodile, although I have seen very few of the latter. Many cameras have been damaged by water in the rapids and the Beaver went to collect Sergeant Ben Cartwright who is an expert instrument repairer, in the hope that he could do something with them. They had not returned by last light.

Because of our growing problem with filtering water I have got two of the engineer section to join the fleet permanently to perform water duties, and I have also brought Major Bill Coleridge, Coldstream Guards, to join the fleet so that I may have a spare helmsman trained in case I have to send one ahead for the reconnaissance of the Stanley Falls. This will leave Major Billy Bowles, 14/20th King's Hussars, in command of FST/C.

The logistic group have decided not to use Air Zaire for the move to Kisangani and this will save money. Instead we shall have to use the more laborious method of rail and river to get our stores forward. In the evening it was discovered that Pam Baker had chicken-pox, undoubtedly caught from her patient earlier in the expedition.

Wednesday 13 November

Night location: Nyangwe 4°14′S, 26°11′E.

Navigation: straightforward, a few shallows, river 600 m wide with current flowing slowly up to 7 km per hour.

Terrain: savannah bush.

Zoology: it was noted that the local people catch relatively few fish probably because they use very wide mesh in their nets. Our scientists using a seine net landed six different species including Nile perch fry, cichlids, and 'sardines'. Two snakes caught while swimming in the river. One, a small cobra, spat its venom at Bob Powell when it was hauled into the recce boat. The other was black with white specks and yellow marking and is of a type unknown to us. Antelope and deer tracks were seen at the camp site. No crocodile, but scorpions in abundance. Monkeys seen in caves and trees on the right bank, but very little bird life at this point.

Entomology: mosquitoes plentiful but not so many of the lace-wings that had almost extinguished our lamps with their numbers on previous nights.

Medical: apart from the one chicken-pox casualty we are all fairly fit. No cases of oncho have been seen locally by the doctors. We hear by radio from FST/B that the roads between Kibombo and Kindu are very bad.

It is getting hotter as we approach the equator and at midday the sun temperature was around 49°C.

This place is where it is alleged Stanley launched the *Lady Alice*. Tomorrow I plan to visit the site and discover what we can of the remains of this historic event. Dr Livingstone also reached this point and spent some months trying to persuade the natives to take him across the river by boat. They would not co-operate and Livingstone was forced to return to the east without being able to trace the course of the river.

There are rumours of one or two historic remains and Richard Snailham, our historian, visited the village tonight and made preparations for us to do a survey tomorrow morning. Captain Kabe, our Zaire naval officer, went with him and it seems the people are friendly and helpful.

During our midday stop Tom Mabe's duck, which he had purchased some time before and had been fattening up to eat, escaped. The recce section eagerly pursued the bird, which fled down river to the cheers of the expedition. By continuously diving the duck got away. Mabe, whose mouth had been watering with expectation, is now very depressed.

Thursday 14 November

We crossed over the river in the early morning aboard the giant inflatable, *David Gestetner*, and several of the recce boats. *David Gestetner* is a very smart craft. She is commanded by Lieutenant John Watkin, flies the White Ensign, and is in the best traditions of the Royal Navy. On the far bank there was a mango grove where it was said Stanley had put together the *Lady Alice* in early November 1876 and then carried her down to the reed-covered hard where he launched her and other canoes on 5 November 1876. An avenue of mango trees, planted about 1887 by Baron Danis in commemoration of the event, was shown to us. We were then shown the house of an eminent Zairois theologian named Professor Dibinga Wa Said, author of books on classical philosophy. We next passed a palm grove where it was said the Arab slavers of Tippu-Tib had lived when Nyangwe was a great commercial and slave trade centre in the last half of the nineteenth century. To the south we could see the site of the house of Sefu, Tippu-Tib's nephew. Nothing remained except the ramparts from which his men defended themselves against the *Force Publique* in 1898. We then proceeded along a winding path for about half a kilometre to a cemetery where we saw the graves of some twelve Belgian soldiers and civilians attached to the *Force Publique*. Their names were inscribed on blue and white enamel plaques. Two of these were still fixed to the slab-like monument but another eight remained with the keeper of the cemetery. These were mostly officers and NCOs killed in the action versus the Arab traders and slavers in the late 1890s. The Arabs eventually fled to Kasongo and slavery retreated. While we were looking at the monument and graves a long, thin, green snake climbed up the monument and rose like some sinister guardian on top of it. I suspect it was a small mamba.

We moved on in the late morning up river eventually camping in equatorial forest at 3°46·2'S, 26°02·2'E. There were many shallows and sand-banks on the journey and the equatorial forest started abruptly at 4°S. It rose like a great green wall from the savannah and was plain to see from several miles away. From here we were to be closed in by the dense greenery until we reached Kinshasa over 1600 kilometres away.

Zoology: we had the best fish catch ever at Nyangwe. One hundred and fifty specimens of twenty different species were caught in one gill net alone! Scorpions and lizard eggs were found in a tree. We suspect these are of a simple gecko type. The eggs were white and oval and approximately eight millimetres long.

Entomology: lace-wings and mosquitoes and flying ants plagued us again.

Temperature: 31°C in the shade and 46°C in the sun at midday.

As dusk fell a very heavy tropical storm struck us with great violence, lasting over an hour. We ate our evening meal in great discomfort but morale remains surprisingly high.

From Stanley's account of Nyangwe it is quite clear that the town was very much larger and more important in those days. I had noticed a certain similarity between the description he gives in *Through the Dark Continent* and what I have seen today. There is some confusion about the question of whether he launched his boats here or not. I believe that in fact he used the *Lady Alice* to cross the river for a sortie on the far side, then returned to Nyangwe, and later marched overland to the north before launching his fleet.

November 5th: Start from Nyangwe North-north-east to Nakasimbi, district of Nyangwe. Marched 9½ miles for 3½ hours.

Hamed Bin Mohammed *alias* Mtibula, or Tippu-Tib, accompanied by nearly 500 souls and over 200 fighting men which added to our party, makes a list of about 700 souls. Muini Kibwana and several young Arabs accompany him. Tippu-Tib is the most dashing and adventurous Arab that has ever entered Africa and to ensure success in this exploration I could not have done better than to have secured his aid in exploring a dangerous country. Few tribes will care to dispute our passage now. I look forward in strong hopes to do valuable exploration. From Nyangwe here travelled over a fine rolling plain-like country, crossed one stream going east.

Friday 15 November

After a wet night we left our forest camp and advanced towards Kindu. The river, now much broken up with large islands, was no great problem. I see from Stanley's map that falls are mentioned in at least one place, but apart from some shallows and sand-banks we had no great problems. The sun soon dried us off and the only problem of the day was water in some of the petrol which gave us engine trouble. One heavy rain shower lasted from 0830 hours to 1030 hours and soaked everything once again. The equatorial forest has now closed right in on both banks of the river. I can imagine the problems that Stanley's party must have had carrying their boats, goods and chattles through this dense forest. According to his diaries, he launched his boats at $3°35'S$, $26°12'E$. I hope to be able to deploy scientists into the equatorial rain forest in the area of Kindu and to allow time for essential repairs to be made to boats, engines and equipment.

Saturday 16 November

In Kindu. Planning and reorganization continues. The scientists, mainly entomologists and botanists, have been deployed to a forest camp to the south of the town. They are very happy with the site and are already hard at work. Local officials are most friendly and have put a number of houses at our disposal. Derek Jackson and his logistic support group are splendidly established with their train and all its carriages loaded with equipment and stores in a siding near the river. I now learn that when the train left Kongolo it started to go the wrong way. Luckily Derek noticed this and managed to persuade the driver to change direction.

I.T.S.O.S.—C

Today the Zairois celebrate Armed Forces Day and many of us were invited to an official dinner at the biggest hotel in the town. It was a very pleasant and enjoyable evening which, following the dinner, became highly informal with the Zairois and expedition members singing songs accompanied by Flight Lieutenant Steve George and Squadron Leader Mike Barnard on their various musical instruments! The town has a somewhat grizzly history from the troubles of the rebellion some years ago and it was very pleasant to find everyone so hospitable now. Much talk of elephant hunting in the region and I was invited to attend a hunt in a few days' time. Ivory and ivory ornaments are in evidence everywhere at reasonable prices.

Stanley's overland journey to this region was far less easy and pleasant.

November 6th: Mpotira. Nyangwe district North ½ East 12 miles.

We had our first experience of the woods, damp and rotting trees and bushes, though there had been no rain.

November 7th: Halt at Mpotira, to allow a winding caravan under our escort to come up with hundreds of sheep and goats which they are taking to Tata for trade. A sheep is said to purchase one ivory, 12 slaves purchase an ivory. In Ujiji six slaves purchase an ivory.

'Slaves cost nothing,' said Hamed Bin Mohammed, 'they only require to be gathered.' And that is the work of Muini Dugumbi and Mtagamoyo.

These half-castes of Nyangwe have no cloth or beads or wares of merchandise. They obtain their ivory by robbing. It is the story of sea pirates and buccaneers over again, of Captain Black the Buccaneer. They attack the simple peoples of Nyangwe right and left, 12 or 15 slaves then caught are sold for 35 pounds of ivory. Muini Dugumbi has 100 to 120 women. Mtagamoyo has 60.

November 8th: North ½ West 9 miles to district of Karindi, Uregga.

We had a fearful time of it today in the woods – such crawling, scrambling, tearing through the damp cool jungles, with such height and depth of woods. Once we got a sidelong view from the limited crown of a hill over the wild woods around us which swept in irregular waves towards the Lualaba and of green grass plains on the other side of Lualaba. It was a wild and weird scene. It was so dark sometimes that I could not see easily the words I wrote in my field book.

November 9th: North $\frac{1}{2}$ West $10\frac{1}{2}$ miles to Kiussi.

Another difficult day's work in the forest and jungle. Our caravan is no longer the tight compact force which was my pride, but utterly disorganised; each one scrambling to the best of his ability through the woods. The boat bearers were utterly wearied out. It may be said that we cut our way through. The Vanguard armed with axes and bill-hooks performed hard work, but to make a road like the pioneers of a governmental army would require many days, as prostrate giants with a mountain of branches and twigs would have to be cut through. To save time we were obliged to cut roads winding round these vast obstructions.

The question which agitates my mind is: whether it would be best to follow the Lualaba to the sea; or follow the Lualaba north until it turns west, and then strike for Munza's thus joining Livingstone's and Schweinfurth's discoveries.

If I struck for the sea, a terrible puzzle presents itself. What shall I do with my people? They would be unable to return overland to Zanzibar and *The Herald* and *Telegraph* would never undertake to incur the expense of sending a party by sea around the Cape. And the glory of crossing Africa would be small for a second party immediately after Cameron's.

On the other hand, by going to Munza's, I resolve the problem of the Lualaba, I round the sources of the Nile and it is better for the interests of my employers; I could discharge my men at Gondoroko and they could return in safety to Zanzibar via Uganda.

However, I leave these questions to be decided definitely until some 30 camps ahead when I must resolve what I mean to do. I must also have an eye for my supplies for they are diminishing rapidly.

The squall heralding rain raises a noise above our heads like that of storm waves driven against rocks.

Sunday 17 November

Visited scientists in forest. Travelling by Land-Rover, had almost reached the camp when Sapper Drake came running up in exhausted state saying he was on his way to get help as Sergeant Mick Hough had just fallen twenty-eight metres from a tree in which he had been fixing light traps for the entomologists. Fortunately, the doctor was with us. Hough was on a roughly made stretcher when we reached him. To me, he looked very dead. To our sheer amazement, within a matter of minutes he recovered and stood up. His language was interesting to say the least, and by some miracle he had broken no bones and appeared to have done relatively little damage to himself. He was put to bed, however, and rested until a full examination of possible injuries could be made. Having examined the site of his fall, I believe it is an absolute miracle that he is alive. By chance, he struck a mound of earth at an angle which tended to lessen the effect of the blow. Had he landed a few centimetres in either direction he would have been impaled on bamboo tree stumps.

Scientists' camp well set up, as one might expect, for it has been largely done by FST/B who, with their complement of Gurkhas, are experts. I discussed their problems with them far into the night, but they were certainly very happy with their present site and are doing excellent work. The evening meal was of monkey, shot by their two Zaire LOs. It had the same rather rank taste as some I had eaten in Darien two years before; not particularly pleasant, but at least it was a filling meal. By radio I heard that our medical team now being established at Kananga are one Range Rover short. Hope to visit them in near future to discuss their problems. Presented scientists with their first bottle of the expedition's Johnny Walker whisky. They eagerly poured out cups of the precious liquid, but – alas – one scientist topped the cups up with formalin instead of water. Terrible despair!

Monday 18 November

Remained with scientists and watched their collecting activities for the rest of the morning. Then returned to Kindu and discussed problem of jet craft that are still in Kinshasa. The difficulty is that we simply cannot get the right sort of fuel – or indeed any sort of fuel in the quantity that these thirsty beasts would require if we were to use them from this point on. Originally I had hoped to introduce the jets at Kongolo, but the fuel problems and the lack of finance has stopped this. I believe now that their most valuable use would be in the final rapids to the west of Kinshasa. Apparently the jet boat team is now coming almost entirely from New Zealand. Originally we were dealing with the English concessionaires for Hamilton Jets, but there is now some confusion as to who exactly we are dealing with. However, I cannot deploy any of our resources to Kinshasa before December and I am anxious that the jet crews should not come to Zaire before then. Tomorrow I hope to talk by radio to the jet boat representative, a Mr George Davidson, who has arrived in Kinshasa.

Much of day spent in discussing logistic problems that lie ahead. Stanley had some seven hundred people moving in a great column through the jungle. I have a far smaller number with a mixture of broken-down Land-Rovers and, when I can get it, a train. I have one light aircraft but fuel is short so I reckon that my problems and Stanley's are not all that different!

The real difficulty that lies ahead is that there is no railway from here to Kisangani. The roads that run to the north are said to be in a very bad state and pass through an area thought to be either held or certainly partially controlled by rebel forces hostile to the Government. Fortunately, the river itself is easily navigable as far as Ubundu (formerly Ponthierville), from where there is a one metre gauge railway to Kisangani. I believe the answer is that we must move the maximum amount of stores by river, using the fleet and hiring some barges. Meanwhile we will need to send a well-prepared overland column to try and get our vehicles through on the bad road. Ernie Durey is clearly the sort of man to lead this. The LOs appear nervous and I have a feeling that they are concerned about the hostile elements ahead of us. It is difficult to know whether we are exaggerating or underestimating these problems. There is a great tendency amongst people here to tell us the sort of news they think we like to hear rather than the complete truth. However, I shall send the fleet on ahead under the command of Mike Gambier and follow myself later when I have solved the problem. I hope to join them at Ubundu by air so that I can be on hand and command the next stretch through the Stanley Falls.

I have already sent FST/A and FST/C ahead to recce this area. There are conflicting stories about the severity of these rapids. Stanley names a total of seven cataracts. Local information is that in the area of Ubundu the river goes underground but I have heard such rumours before. This was the one stretch that our recce party in 1971–72 could not examine carefully. As far as I can tell, there are bad sets of rapids at the beginning and end, with one or two minor rapids in between. I suspect we shall have to portage at least once in this area.

One small worry is the time it has taken for mail to reach us from Britain, and indeed there does seem to be a fair amount of mail going astray. Another problem with the mail is that some of the photographers' film going back to England is found to be fogged, and this is thought to be due to X-rays being taken as part of the security operations for examining mail for letter bombs. Morale is still generally high and I attribute much of this to our excellent rations. Certainly those responsible in the Ministry of Defence victualling department, and also our sponsors, have done a magnificent job in providing these delicacies for us. We are likewise indebted to local sponsors who kindly produce so much for us, including beer. Fruit is plentiful and the avocado pears are excellent.

I have noticed that the people in this region are variously clad in everything from loin-cloths to European type of dress. Some of them still wear copper bracelets which appear to be quite old. I have also been shown some rather old money in various shapes including an H and a cross. It is made of copper. I have noticed this appearing all the way down the river from Bukama.

In general all the people are very friendly and our Zaire LOs are doing everything possible to look after our interests.

Tuesday 19 November

Stanley had experienced a great many more difficulties in this region. For days he had struggled through the difficult country with his porters lagging seriously behind and the jungle getting thicker.

November 12th: Halt.

It has been decided to abandon the right bank of the Lualaba, there is no food sufficient for our force to be found in the jungles and the jungle forest is too dense to make way. However, for 18 camps ahead I have obtained a pretty correct knowledge. We shall follow the Lualaba on the left bank. Boat came today, people utterly fagged out and disheartened.

November 13th: Wenekamankua North ¼ West 4 miles.
Still woods, woods, woods.

November 14th: Marched to Wane-Mbeza, Uregga. 8 miles still through the forest North-West.

Uregga it seems runs like a broad belt from north-north-east to south-south-west. Its people know nothing beyond three camps on either side. Many of them have not even seen the Lualaba River, though they are but 30 miles off. The most incurious people ever met. They have been imprisoned for generations in their woods, and the difficulty of making way through these forests which surround them is the sole cause why they know nought of the world outside or the world outside knows aught of them. It appears to be synonymous with the Forest Country.

Woods and deep ravines with an outlook towards the north and north-east of a world of hills and ranges of the most portentous and forbidding kind. To add to our toilsome situation, Hamed Bin Mohammed, labouring uneasily under his contract, first found fault with the length of the marches, and then wished to bind me down with a promise that at the end of 60 camps I should give him one half of my force to enable him to return to Nyangwe, whether I saw means or not of being able to proceed towards the confluence of the Lualaba and the Coango.

As this was sheer nonsense to reduce my force in the middle of the wilderness, without the slightest prospect of overcoming the difficulty of proceeding to fulfil my mission, the proposal was not entertained but I endeavoured to keep him within the terms of the agreement. This he refused to do, because after escorting me so far he would be afraid to return alone with only his own people. The natives – he said – would suspect he had fought in some country and they would, roused by cupidity or blood-thirstiness, set on us with the cry 'Lets finish them!' No, he could not think of it. 'Give me,' said he, '30 or 35 guns and men at the end of 60 camps and I will go with you that distance.'

While I wished him to proceed according to the contract, on the promise that I should meet with a Portuguese caravan, I should give him 30 or 35 guns and men, while I should proceed with 15 or 20 men on my way; or if at the end of 60 camps, provided such distance approached anywhere near the confluence of the two rivers Coango and Lualaba, if he would wait, I would leave half my goods in his possession and with my force I would push on rapidly to where the two rivers flowed and contented with the work done would return with him to Nyangwe, and thence to Zanzibar. No, the Arab, whose mind was bent on breaking the agreement or making money, refused to listen. He seemed bent on making the marches as short as possible by delays and needless waits on the road, so that the 60 marches would not indeed amount to more than 30 ordinary marches.

It is not always easy to follow Stanley's account because many of the names of places and rivers have changed in the last hundred years, but his descriptions of the terrain are just as applicable today. He continued to march parallel to the river.

November 17th: Still woods – most frightful work. We have left Uregga, and entered Uvinza or Uzimba, who wear caps of monkey skin, heavy red copper rings round ankles. Weapons: a short bladed spear, a knife and small bows which shoot poisoned arrows: bows are not more than about a foot in length, for they are only to wound at short distance. The slightest wound occasions death if blood drawn, powerful poison. A variety of trees and shrubs, perfectly wonderful. The cotton woods serve for boards to make doors. They carve long benches, low stools. Red woods also abundant and a tough black wood resembling ebony forms the favourite spear staff. Village of Kampunzu is about 500 yards long, one street 30 feet wide forms the village, clay walls. Waregga use wattled wall.

Blood brotherhood is a sure sign of peace. This was made between Frank Pocock and the Chief, and interchanged presents. Women of Uregga and Uzimba are naked. Men wear a loin clout of bark cloth or grass cloth. The bark cloth tree is almost a sure indication of the duration of each settlement. In Uganda, where peace is ensured by force and numbers, they grow to a great size hundreds of years old. But in all these sections I have failed to see trees more than 30 or 40 years old.

November 19th: March 5 miles West to Lualaba River East long. 26° 12′ S. Lat. 3° 35′.

Arrived at river – which is divided into two broad streams 60 yards wide by a series of small wooded islands – we began to screw up the boat and make arrangements for crossing. We endeavoured, before they were aware we had a boat, to bargain for canoes, but such obtuse-headed fellows jeered us, requested us to give them a heap of shells a cubit high, which would have been about 140 pounds. We proceeded quietly with our work and suddenly launched the boat amid shouts, and manning her with 25 rifles appeared behind the islands in front of the Wagenya settlements and proceeding close to the bank commanded them to appear at camp before sunset to make friends, or we should make war on them. By 5 p.m. we had crossed 150 men into the island in front from the eastern bank. This fact, it seems, acted on the natives with greater force for they at once appeared with canoes to assist the crossing. Had we not had the boat we should have had to wait a month.

At Kampunzu's we saw what appeared to us each street or village lined with human skulls. One had 26, another 10, another 13, which made us first imagine Kampunzu as a terrible fighter, but we were told they were Sokos' or gorillas' skulls singularly resembling humanity – 4½ feet high, the size of a lad of 14 or thereabouts. Hair black brown and long. I offered Kampunzu a high price if he would show me one dead or alive, but though he beat the drum and started scores off to hunt, he was unsuccessful.

November 20th: Crossed Lualaba at Rukonbeh's, 458 souls, 4 asses and about 150 loads of beads and cloth etc. etc. The natives could not be induced to assist, and we had to take canoes by force. No violence was however used. Notwithstanding we offered high prices for food, natives ran away abandoning everything.

November 21st: Halt.

We have used all the diplomacy in our power to induce the natives to be friends, but it has been of no use. Two of my people went to purchase food. The natives sold food but in the meantime surrounded them and one of them threw a spear at Kacheche, who shot him dead. There is not a native within 10 miles of us.

For the rest of November 1876 Stanley continued to move his expedition north along the river. As many as possible floated in the boats while a large land party moved parallel to them along the bank. The jungle was still thick and difficult, the people were growing steadily more hostile, and food does not seem to have been easy to obtain for his large group.

November 25th: Crossed the Ruiki R. with the Expedition. A little before it arrived, a tragedy took place. A foolish old man persisted in advancing to the canoes to repossess himself of one, and being repeatedly driven off by main force, finally advancing with a spear and cheered by a mob on the other side of the Ruiki, one of my boy gun-bearers lifted up a rifle and shot him in the heart. I unfortunately was absent, having gone up the Lualaba to meet the Expedition, or I might have saved the foolish but determined old man.

November 27th: Floated down Rualaba about 4 miles, came to place near Lukassa Rapids.

View between the Ruiki and Nakanpemba

Natives extremely insolent, had a brush, two natives killed.
West end of hilly ridge seen from Nakanpemba. We came to rapids
and falls, steered close inshore and made all fast.

With 10 men I started down the left bank to explore, leaving
orders for Frank Pocock and men not to stir until my return. In
the woods found natives preparing ambuscades below the second
rapids, some of the oldest directing some of the younger warriors
where to conceal themselves. Canoes were also being hidden in
small cove with paddles nearby. We found all this out on first
hearing voices and concealing ourselves, and their manoeurvres
were plainly revealed. A mile lower down were a fleet of about
50 canoes, engaged in shifting things from the main land to the
island on whose either side several rapids were. We opened the
ball, and soon ousted the ambuscade, and some sheep were seized
as spoil of the victors. We also made the island too hot to hold
them, as in our operations of clearing the several rapids it was
most undesirable to have an enemy lurking in the grass or reeds
below the rapids.

On returning from the rendezvous, I was alarmed on hearing
that Frank Pocock had permitted four of my best men to shoot
the rapids in canoes, upon which I nothing doubted some
calamity, as we had witnessed the hostile manoeuvres of the
natives. After sending ten men down left bank, I was rejoiced to

hear the men though chased had escaped, but regretted to hear that three Snyders were lost. The foolish people had shot two rapids, but at the third were upset and only one of the four managed to save his rifle. They had been swept into a whirlpool, sucked in, taken to the bottom and shot to surface some feet below the pool. Sitting astride of their canoes they were chased by the natives, but one revolver and rifle saved them. They paddled to land with their hands and were soon discovered and rescued by the land party.

Tonight we are camped below the first rapids on the left bank with noise of falling and rushing water all around us.

Stanley's advance continued, and to add to his difficulties there was an outbreak of smallpox among his land-based party. One of the casualties was Tippu-Tib's concubine who died on 15 December. On 18 December he reached a place named Vinya-Njara. This I deduced to be either the actual site of, or very close to, the modern town of Kindu.

December 18th: We came from Kisui Kachiambi to Kisunga's market place. Halted a short while to enable land party to reach us. Not coming, sent a small party West to hunt up news of them. This party arrived before a village where spears were thrown at them, and in turn they made a clean sweep of the village and captured a woman and child which they brought to me. By means of these captives I succeeded in checking the demonstrativeness of the Mpika Island people and inducing them to refrain from indulging in war. We made peace and brotherhood with them, and the news spread quickly, and we heard shouts of 'Go in peace'. Then descending the river we came to Vinya-Njara where we made preparations to camp. After clearing out a landing place, the people began to stir about to prepare food. While digging peanuts, a shower of arrows continue until night and the next morning the arrows fell, when, perceiving we had sufficient cause to begin war, we made a stockade, built three stockades on three ant hills commanding the village, sent out scouts to the forest . . . At noon I went in a canoe to get the latitude and by means of field glasses discovered the nest whence the arrows came; descending a short distance until I came within range, I took aim and succeeded in dropping a Chief . . .

December 20th : Halt.

Made a night expedition and captured 4 canoes. Sent a land expedition to search for the enemy, wounded one man. I killed one yesterday who was probably a Chief or an influential person for the weeping and sorrow was great and since then they have become utterly unnerved.

At this point Tippu-Tib and his men were also unnerved and refused to continue with Stanley. He had no choice but to release them. After a cheerful Christmas Day he presented gifts to the infamous slaver and prepared to advance north with his own people alone. Having dispensed with his slow-moving land party he should be able to move more quickly, which was as well because from now on he would have to defend himself. Speed might well be essential.

Wednesday 20 November

Our boats departed at 1200 hours after a photographic session with much overflying by the Beaver. The remainder of the support group and Tac HQ spent the day in sticking stamps on to the special envelopes that we are preparing for philatelists all over the world. It is a long and arduous job which has already occupied much of our time at other stops on this journey. I trust that the stamp collectors who wait so eagerly for them will appreciate the problems that we had to endure in carrying out this task. Stanley would certainly have laughed at the thought of expeditions having to devote so much time to fund-raising even in the field.

More discussion with Kinshasa over the radio regarding the jet boats. Decided to launch a jet boat recce of the Livingstone Falls in early December. This will be earlier than planned but I think it will be valuable and the jet boat team seem very anxious to get on with this and do something. However, I have warned them that I can give no real support until late December at the earliest. I find now that through their generosity, the Zaire Army have provided us with too many LOs. Although we needed them in the early stages of our deployment they are now a problem. Because of our shortage of fuel and transport it has not been possible to deploy as widely as I would have wished and so there is not the need for so many LOs to accompany parties. I have also heard that some twelve Zaire scientists are about to arrive to join in the expedition. They are of course very welcome, and it will be interesting to meet them, but as yet I have no idea which disciplines they represent and what research they wish to undertake. However, it is an encouraging sign that the Zaire Government are so interested in the project as to send some of their best men to join us.

A group of our own scientists are returning to Britain at this stage, having completed their work. With them goes Dorothy Bovey who has done splendidly as the botanical illustrator. The sight of Dorothy striding through the jungle with paints and a long dress, treating the whole exercise in many ways as if it was a stroll in a Surrey woodland, has caused many a moment of mirth. She is a most determined person and her work, good humour and cheerfulness has been much appreciated. Jeremy Mallinson, the Director of the Jersey Wild Life Conservation Trust, is also returning. He has been our expert on primates and was fortunate to spend five days a few weeks ago in the company of some eleven gorillas in the hills to the north-east. He believes that he has some splendid photographs of one angry but fortunately bluffing gorilla charging him!

Our farthest-flung party remains Chimp Force who report they are progressing satisfactorily although so far they have not tracked down the elusive pygmy chimpanzee. We recently sent them a parachute drop of supplies but they are keen to get a small outboard motor for their Avon rubber boat which I will now have to try to find from one of the FSTs.

The news from London is pretty gloomy. Britain seems to be going through a particularly bad time and our funds are very low, if they exist at all! I know our friends at the

Ministry of Defence are working hard but we desperately need a little more money, otherwise this expedition will grind to a halt. Maximum economy being exercised by all parties.

Mike Gambier reports the fleet's position tonight at 0·2°43·5'S, 25°52·5'E. They have sailed thirty-two kilometres. There is no change in the terrain or bank composition. They are continuing to collect water samples and the zoologists have been laying fish nets. They report that a female dik-dik has been brought into their camp, the animal is about two months old and has been badly hurt in a trap.

The fleet stopped for the night and camped in a palmoil factory. Only half the factory working. Local chief did not know they were coming, but despite his surprise was very friendly.

General observations: accuracy of 1:250 000 maps highly suspect. Many islands misplaced and some not even shown. River fairly shallow as shown by many twists and turns in marked channel.

Thursday 21 November

Boats continue to advance. FST/C is at Kisangani. FST/A is at Ubundu and FST/B is at Kindu with my Tac HQ and the support group. Plans working very well at the moment.

A local house-boy employed by Tac HQ seems to have been guilty of a little underhand play. Two of our liaison sergeants nicknamed Tact and Persuasion dealt with him very effectively! The Zaire LOs are extremely loyal to us and do a great deal to look after our welfare. A little time ago at Kongolo a local thief stole a battery from us, but was spotted by a boy who reported the matter to the LOs. They seized the man and beat him thoroughly before dragging him off to a magistrate. On the way he was stoned by the crowd and eventually the wretched fellow received one year in prison for his sins. Because of the kindness and hospitality shown to us in that town I sent a plea for mercy and had the sentence reduced to six months' penal servitude.

Recently some students started to taunt our work-boys who were helping with the train. They were criticizing them for working for white men. Almost immediately two gendarmes appeared and beat the offenders soundly.

It seems a strange world that here in the middle of Africa we have so many friends. I plan to fly down to see the medical research team at Kananga tomorrow. I fear they are so far away that it will be difficult for us to give them the right support but I hope to be able to visit them once or twice during the expedition. It would also be interesting to see a new area of country for we shall pass over both vast stretches of tropical rain forest and also much savannah.

The fleet is reported to be at 2°16'S, 25°46'E. Distance covered: 51 km. The river is as before but with more sandy stretches. There is no change in the bank composition. The Elila River (a tributary) is a soft-water river, as opposed to the Lualaba which is hard water.

Zoology: one as yet unidentified species of cichlid caught in overnight net by entrance of Elila River. One eight-foot crocodile seen on driftwood midstream five kilometres south of this location. One palm-nut eagle seen and a few terns. The bird life is increasing slightly. There were a great many weaver birds, the first we had seen since the Bukama area.

The people of Monganda fled on first seeing the recce section. (Who would not!) Lieutenant Somue persuaded them to return. The fleet are the first white faces they have seen since 1960. They speak Songola. Mike Gambier reports that the map is now very unreliable.

Friday 22 November

Flew down this morning with Pam Baker to visit Freddie Rodger and his medical team at Kananga. Long flight over top of rain forest. Saw surprisingly little game while passing over savannah. With such lush grassland I would

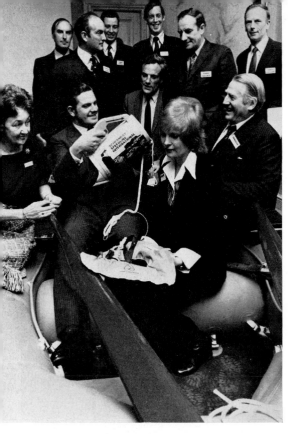

Left: Pre-expedition press conference at the offices of Colman, Prentis and Varley, one of our sponsors. *L to r (sitting):* Kay Thompson, J. B–S, Mike Gambier, Pam Baker, Freddie Rodger, *(standing):* Richard Snailham, Ernie Durey, Peter Marett, Paul Arengo-Jones, Jim Masters, Dick Festorazzi

Below: J. B-S gives his first briefing at Kolwezi. Among the audience are Capt Kabe, Zaire Navy (arms folded, dark beret), and Capt Kayalo, Zaire Army (hands on hips)

Left: Shooting the first rapid in an Avon Professional. *L to r:* Richard Snailham, Jim Masters, John Connor, Bob Russell

Below: Rev Basil Pratt, RAChD, holds a service near the source of the Zaire

Opposite top: Jim Masters rowing an Avon Professional in calm conditions. Note the Johnson $4\frac{1}{2}$ hp outboard on the stern

Opposite below: Avon Professional in rough water between the dams on 19 October

Left: Paddington Falls at the start of the Red Gorge. Polaroid photograph taken on a recce by Capt Peter Marett

Centre: Lunch at Crocodile Pool on 19 October.
L to r: Eric Rankin, J. B-S, Pam Baker, Peter Marett, Charles Horsfall, Chief Wakipindgi and Lt Bonguele (Zaire LO)

Below: Giant inflatables near Kongolo
L to r: David Gestetner (nearest camera), *La Vision, Barclays Bank.* An Avon S400 is alongside *Barclays Bank*

Opposite top: The 'admiral's bridge' on *La Vision.* Dr John Chapman-Smith sits on the bow. Note cooking firewood being carried in Avon Professional alongside to save precious fuel. Lucas head-lamps are for night navigation

Opposite below: The fleet on the river in line ahead: *La Vision, Barclays Bank, David Gestetner*

Left: At work on *La Vision*'s bridge. *L to r:* Sqn Ldr Mike Barnard RAF (navigator), Richard Snailham (with beard) writing notes for his book, J. B-S writing log, Peter Marett keeping an eye on way ahead

Centre: The train in Kindu. *L to r:* Two English students, Maj Gordon Mitchell, L.Cpl Tom Sim, Capt Peter Marett

Below: Maggie Bush (centre) helps with the washing

Right: Dr Roger Sweeting
with Biggles and Cromwell

Centre: Entomologists' collection
displayed by Dr Stephen Sutton.
Jerry Pass (TV film team),
Mike Gambier in background

Below: An encounter with an
adult male mountain gorilla
in bamboo forest in NE Zaire

Above: The accident at Ubundu. *La Vision* goes down the hole

Left: Avon Professional shooting the final cataract of the Stanley Falls. Fish traps in background

have expected to see cattle, but even they were absent.

Landed at Kananga and after a little difficulty with local officials eventually met up with Lieutenant Mike Rowlatt of the Parachute Regiment who took us by Range Rover out to visit base camp of research team at Dimbelenge. Beaver meanwhile followed by air and eventually landed at convenient airstrip near medical base. Research team, which consists of Belgians, French, Zairois and Britons, were working some way from base so not possible to actually see them at work in field. Spent evening with them and discussed their many problems. Certain amount of division over administrative matters and one of the bones of contention was the driving of the four Range Rovers provided by the Zaire Government.

The research team base is a small cottage and nothing like as good as the houses we are being loaned on the river. Nevertheless, their work is going ahead as planned. There was no radio contact this evening, and indeed their A14 radio is having difficulty in getting through over such a long distance. Freddie Rodger himself is working with his usual energy and seems to be almost indefatigable.

On the river the fleet reached 1°51·7'S, 25°49'E. Distance covered: 47 km.

Terrain: ground and bank composition, no change.

Water: collecting continues. River much cleaner.

Zoology: crocodile sighted at 1000 hours, approximately two and a quarter metres long. It was swimming in midstream and submerged on boat's approach. During night, family of chimpanzees visited fleet's camp but retired after ten minutes. At lunchtime, near village of Putu, another chimpanzee surprised an expedition member who was communing with nature! A Polypterus, about a metre in length, was found by fish team in overnight net.

Medical: one case of conjunctivitis.

The local people are members of Lokege tribe. The river is well marked and has obviously been used frequently for navigation by local craft.

Saturday 23 November

Bad weather in early morning delayed flight back. Eventually took off 1330 hours and flew back over swamp and primary forest. Saw ten elephants moving in thin jungle beneath us and filmed them. Noticed that much vegetation had been burnt off and this had resulted in growth of inedible grass; perhaps this accounts for lack of cattle and game. Noticed there were very few birds about. A fascinating area to fly over.

We are changing over medical officers with the logistic group. Ian Young has gone home and gynaecologist Dr Vyvyan (Viv) Jones joins us at Kisangani. Meanwhile Derek Jackson has been stitching up various natives wounded in bar fights.

Fleet's position now 1°25'S, 25°51'E. Distance covered: 48 km.

Terrain: vegetation now includes more palm trees. River banks becoming difficult to penetrate except in places where locals clear landing points, on account of mud and thick elephant grass.

Water: level of river has risen in last forty-eight hours. The consistency at this point (Lowa) is more muddy. The water's chemistry will be studied tomorrow.

Zoology: a crocodile sighted midstream two kilometres down the Alowa.

Fleet now pauses for thirty-six hours. Natives friendly and have invited expedition to visit their festivities.

Sunday 24 November

Am conferring with local people regarding okapi, a rare type of giraffe found only in Zaire. I decided it would be of great interest to see in wild state. After discussions with local authorities I believe best answer is to send recce party eastward from Kisangani to seek out the beast. Therefore, today I flew north to Kisangani with Pam Baker, having briefed her on the work to be done. On way we made air drop of mail to fleet who were at work at the Lowa junction. Also visited FST/A who were situated at small airstrip to north of Ubundu. They were in good heart and gave us a small Johnson outboard motor for Chimp Force.

At Kisangani talked with FST/C who seemed in high spirits and were doing well. It was first time I had seen city, if only from air, and I was also able to examine Stanley Falls. First impression is that they are not as formidable as reported and we should be able to get through without portage.

The TV team flew on to Kananga today for two days with medical research team. This evening we held party for local people in Kindu.

Monday 25 November

Final preparations now made for move from Kindu. Scientists naturally reluctant to leave such productive area early but the show must move on. Lunch today with Monsieur L'Abbé, Catholic missionary of this area. Interesting man who kindly gave me fine ivory head.

Fleet reported new position: 00°48′S, 25°32′E. Distance covered: 60 km.

Water: the Lowa is markedly cooler than the Lualaba River. The Lowa is the faster-flowing river with soft water and a great deal of mud in suspension.

Zoology: a labeo fish was caught after a small bank had been blasted with explosive by engineers. A two-year-old pygmy chimpanzee (*Pan Paniscus*) was seen as a pet in a house near Lowa. First living specimen we have seen! Understand it came from Kindu area.

Fleet still experiencing trouble with maps. Navigator, Squadron Leader Mike Barnard, reports current has increased to 5 km per hour. Fleet sails on to Ubundu at 1430 hours tomorrow.

Although the Zairois are very kind to us I much prefer to

avoid the towns. Because of all the diplomatic and administrative difficulties and the need for me to be in close touch
with Zairois authorities, I must usually accept the houses
that they press on us for my Tac HQ. The advantage is
that it gives me better overall control of the expedition and
allows me a certain amount of privacy to deal with the
delicate problems that arise almost hourly. But it does
mean that I tend to be a little out of touch with the members
of the fleet who are normally accommodated elsewhere.
The problem is that with such a large party we simply
cannot all be based in one place when we are in a town; this
is only possible when in the jungle.

Tuesday 26 November

Flew to airstrip known as Kilometre 95 this morning. It is
one and a half hours by Land-Rover to north of Ubundu.
On the way to Ubundu in the half-light we came upon a
group of large apes; appeared much bigger than captive
chimpanzee and for a moment I thought they were gorillas.
Stopped to investigate and followed them up, pistol in
hand just in case, but was pretty certain they were chimpanzees.

On arrival at Ubundu we held an O group and also
celebrated Jim Master's twenty-fifth wedding anniversary,
with an excellent cake made by one of our nurses, Adrianne
Damgaard. Flight enabled me to do good recce of the
Ubundu section of Stanley Falls. On close inspection I do
not think it is quite as easy as we make out. Beaver was late
going back and I was somewhat concerned that it should
reach its base at Kindu before nightfall, as an especially
heavy tropical storm was raging to the south. A problem for
a single-engined aircraft in this land is that there is little
hope of diverting to another airfield if one is rained or
weathered out. Fuel is also in short supply and flying altogether a pretty hazardous business in Zaire at the moment.
There were one of two minor political problems to be sorted

out when I reached Ubundu, but in general people had once again been helpful and fleet was in good order. Tomorrow we shall reorganize here, transfer surplus stores to the train to be sent north, and then with boat suitably lightened start to tackle Stanley Falls.

Wednesday 27 November

Spoke today to Chimp Force who seemed to be doing well on their river, although still no sign of pygmy chimpanzees. Bob Hudson reports that they are suffering from jiggers which have buried deep into their feet.

Peter Knudsen, one of our doctors who has been doing an especially fine job with the local people, has been recalled to his hospital in Denmark and must leave us. This is a sad blow.

FST/A have been carrying out the reconnaissance of the river and banks in this sector. I studied their reports in detail today and feel fairly confident about the first part of our journey north from Ubundu. However, there is some tricky water in the initial stretch. The video film has been particularly useful once again. What a splendid invention this is. I foresee a great future for it.

Sapper Major John Benham-Crosswell's party ran into some trouble at Wanie Rukula. Their guide was beaten up by local people who thought he was a spy for another tribe. The group had to beat a hasty retreat to escape from a tense situation.

Had long discussion with Mike Gambier. The scientific work carried out during their voyage north from Kindu has obviously been most productive. In addition the Zaire anthropologist, Citoyen Kagabo, has been studying the people along the banks. He has come across the pygmies who live in this area and have in some cases intermarried with the other Africans. The result of one such marriage lives in the village of Lokele. He is a man of about forty so this practice is by no means a new phenomenon.

It has proved very useful to have a Zairois anthropologist working with us because the people along this stretch of the river are definitely frightened by white faces. On first seeing the fleet they nearly always flee. Few white men have visited this area since 1960. At Lowa members of the expedition attended a service in the local church. Many people came out of curiosity to see what was undoubtedly the largest party of white people in the area for many years. A little agriculture, some palm oil manufacture and fishing seem to be the sum total of the industry in this region.

On their way north the fleet has passed the *Ulindi* (originally the *Baron de Cuvelier*), a river steamer built in Newcastle upon Tyne in 1923. There was so much firewood stacked around the upper deck that there appeared to be little or no room for passengers. This is one of the few river steamers still in operation in this area. During the day we purchased stamps from the local post office for use on our special envelopes. There we noticed many old-age pensioners waiting for their quarterly payment of 50 zaires (approximately £45). Fleet temporarily accommodated in warehouse alongside rail terminal. Local railway officials most helpful. Noise of frogs croaking makes sleep difficult.

Dined with Father Augustine at mission. Told us in somewhat scathing terms of a recent visit by some English people who were canoeing parts of the river. He alleges that they sponged off his mission and two other establishments, and we had to do what we could to make amends for our countrymen. Father Augustine was the only survivor from when the mission was attacked during the Simba revolt. He had been away on leave at the time and returned to find everyone had been killed. An interesting evening during which we learnt much about the local area including reports of crude oil seeping from the ground nearby.

Completed refuelling and preparation of fleet by last light. Final briefing given in great detail thanks to work of FST/A and Peter Marett. Video and Polaroid films most useful. One or two of our people now sick including John

Benham-Crosswell and Corporal Brian Sanders, RE, who have malaria.

River over a kilometre and a half wide at this point, but shortly to be constricted as it enters the Stanley Falls, of which I learn there are seven cataracts over some seventy kilometres.

On 28 December 1876 Stanley had said farewell to Tippu-Tib and rode away down-river.

December 30th: We made but four miles today owing to rainy weather and a storm. The morning was passed on the shore of Luru or Lulu where natives of Iryamba made friends with us and sold us a few bananas and palm butter. At about 2 pm in the afternoon the rain having ceased, we pulled across to Iryamba when a storm arose in the crossing and two heavily loaded river canoes sank; two men were drowned . . . and 4 guns were lost, which makes 7 guns lost in this river. I fear this disaster would cause the people to rebel and return, but I was cheered to hear that they deemed it nothing more than Fate, and if Fate had ordained that we should perish, to return or proceed would present no escape. It was therefore better to go on, said the Chiefs. We have had omens and sayings plentiful enough to forbid our further progress, but down-river has such charm that we are compelled to go on. I hope to God that there are no tremendous cataracts ahead; with steep hills on each side of the river, such a place would indeed be a chasm.

December 31st: Continue the journey down river to uninhabited island 182 geographical miles North $\frac{1}{2}$ East from Nyangwe.

Journey today though not long was prosperous, the day fine. Island near the Iryamba, north, very populous and large, natives belligerent. Made tactics for a naval fight but changed their minds prudently and retired without exchange of hurtful salutes. I find it terrible trouble to take charge of so many people totally innocent of anything approaching to manliness or sense on water. It is one protracted torture, chest aches with violent shouting and upbraiding them for their foolish cowardice, voice becomes hoarse with giving orders which in a few seconds are entirely forgotten.

I have 143 souls, men, women and children, two riding asses, 2 goats and 1 sheep.

Out of these 143, 107 are enlisted men in my employ for wages. Out of these 107 only 48 have guns.

Out of these 48 only 32 are effective men who would be able to make a tolerable resistance.

Add to these 32 men, myself and Frank Pocock, and we are 34 fighting men, 109 are mere dummies which serve to frighten off savages deterred by a show of heads rather than arms.

They are terribly dull people to lead across Africa. They smoke *banghy* till they literally fall down half smothered. It took me nearly 2 years to teach my boatmen how to row a boat and to take charge of her. After 2 years practice, one fellow, Muscati, loaded his gun with paper and a bullet and was surprised that his gun did not fire. On nearing an island, I shouted out to one of my boatmen, Rojab, to seize the branches of a tree to prevent us being swept from the landing by the current. 'Yes, sir,' he shouted, and jumped on land and seized the bushes; while the boat was swept away leaving him on the island. At one landing I shouted, when about to continue our journey, to push away. Muscati stood in his canoe, bent his back double, seized his canoe pushing away manfully and was surprised when his canoe did not budge. Muini Hassan, Captain of a canoe, being told to punt his canoe up into a creek, called one of his crew to assist him. His man punted all right, but the Captain braced his pole forward against his man, and finding his canoe was obstinate, scolded his man heartily for about 5 minutes, who had to continue against strong currents and the Captain's punting pole.

January 1st 1877: Continue the journey from uninhabited island to Kerembuka. The journey was mostly through uninhabited forests, except that there was one large settlement on island and mainland. Until today we were called Wasambye. We were today called Wajiwa and our guns called *katadzi* while before they were called *kibongeh* or lightning. We were gliding gently down past the settlement and attempting in mild terms to make specific overtures, addressed as Friends, and greeted them with the words *Sen-nen-neh* or 'Peace'. We got no answer although we saw them plainly enough behind the plantains and trees, crouching with drawn bows. We passed them by. Then our gentle and quiet behaviour was regarded by them as cowardice, and their wooden war drums were beaten and immediately 14 canoes well manned dashed out from the creeks and the islands, others following in full chase after us, loaded with shouting crews, and with them broad shields – door-like. I at once anchored in midstream, while the canoes took shelter along an islet sheltered by overhanging mangrove. I awaited some time to allow the natives to advance. They floated down to 300 yards of the boat and halted their canoes on the mainland. I aimed at the nearmost canoe and fortunately struck two with the first bullet, at the sight of which they all precipitated themselves into the water and cried out: 'Let them go, before we are all exterminated. These people will not be stopped. Let them go, we are dead.' Before this they were saying: 'We shall eat Wajiwa today.'

Such fools it is hardly possible to imagine as these. At one place, Ikondu, they set nets to catch us, and one was shot in the act of setting a large game net. They considered us as game to be trapped, shot, or bagged at sight.

January 2nd: Continue the journey down river to Katumbi.

Today has been a lively day without stop at Lombo-a-Kiriro, we made friends, and permitted 4 large canoes, one about 90 feet long manned with 35 paddlers, to pass by with a peaceful salutation. After giving the word 'Peace', and going down a little, we saw we were followed by them and others coming from Kibombo Island and Amu Nyam. It seemed to me that we were about to have a busy time. I do not wait to be surrounded, but at once dropped anchor and opened fire, while the canoes were sent ashore to do damage. The people seeing we were not to be victims as they had intended, ran away, and we seized eatables and canoes and captured 2 women. One we have released to carry a message of peace to her friends, with a promise that if they make peace we shall release the other, as we are not come for war but to see the river. At Katumbi about dusk a native was seen thrusting a spear into the camp. About 6 natives fell today in the passage down river.

January 3rd: Continue journey from Katumbi down Rowwa river to the Baswa Banki rapids.

We began the journey pleasantly enough. About 3 miles below Katumbi we came to a great number of low islands, separated from the right bank by a narrow stream which we descended. We soon came to a number of canoes, some dozen in number, whose crews were terribly frightened. Greeting them peacefully they loudly responded to our cry of peace, and we passed on followed by several of them who received permission to indulge their curiosity. For three hours our descent was not marred, and we hoped that a day so auspiciously begun would end so, but at Mwana-Ntaba where we left a boy and a woman in a canoe loaded with food to pass unmolested, our pleasure was soon turned to war. Drums, horns, cries along the banks summoned the people to arms, who presently appeared with shields and spears to interrupt our descent.

For two hours we fought with them at the end of which, finding they had retired, we continued our descent as far as the Mikonju River. Mwana-Ntaba ends at the south bank of the Mikonju and the country of the Baswa tribe begins who soon manifested their aversion to strangers by challenging us and coming up from the islands in the Rapids to us. On rounding the point at the north bank of the Mikonju we soon saw the reason for their ferocity in the Rapids, which was an obstacle to delay us and to give them an opportunity to test our prowess and courage. We accepted the challenge after peace was refused, and a few rounds sent them flying. Near the Rapids on the right bank we constructed a strong camp. Elephants very numerous by recent tracks. Slept undisturbed save by shrill weird cries of the lemur and gorilla.

So it was that both expeditions arrived in the same area at about the same time of year.

Thursday 28 November

Night location: 00°15'S, 25°32·5'E. Distance covered: 22 km.

Terrain: tropical rain forest, having passed through what are known locally as Tshungu rapids. I note that Stanley referred to these as the Baswa rapids. They are the first cataract of the Stanley Falls.

I had been forewarned of the possibility of some hostility on the part of the local people here. Not everyone in these parts is particularly favourably disposed towards the government. Accordingly, I have made one or two changes to our deployment and have distributed arms so that we continue to appear to be a very strong and well prepared force. We have kept a very close eye on the jungle at the edges of the river.

The rapids themselves were certainly not easy. The first part of the journey was no great problem but quite suddenly, without warning, one of the leading reconnaissance boats plunged into an abyss, going down into a great hole on the far side of an enormous boulder over which a torrent of water was cascading. Unable to stop or divert, the flagship, *La Vision*, plunged after it. We were hardly prepared for such an event and the engine immediately cut out as it was drowned. Water swept over the craft and we were hurled about by giant waves from all sides. Ken Mason, the *Daily Telegraph* photographer, unfortunately lost some of his cameras which had been lashed down in the fore compartment; the force of the water smashed the rope which was holding them. Eventually we were flung out of the hole, leaving behind the mountains of water pouring into it from all sides. Apart from cuts and bruises and a loss of equipment there was no damage. But we were certainly very shaken. The next boat, *Barclays Bank*, managed to skirt round the left side of the hole; but the last one, *David Gestetner*, also plunged into the abyss and was hurled right up on to its bow with its stern almost standing vertically in the air. There it teetered for a moment before crashing back, fortunately on its hull, and the helmsman managed to get it out. One of the recce boats also went in, having lost all engine-power and the whole fleet had an extremely lucky escape. Some time spent afterwards in collecting bits of equipment floating in the river.

While we were engaged in this operation one very large python (approximately six metres long with yellow and dark brown markings) was seen swimming in the area. Otherwise, wild life was scarce though I saw many fish traps and the local villagers are all fishermen. There were small groups of people at the river's edge, and I noticed with a little apprehension that most of them were armed with bows, arrows and spears. The bows, however, were of a small variety that would probably have little effect against us unless the arrows are poisonous. The spears carried were the short, stabbing variety and are clearly not made for long-distance throwing. None of the natives carried firearms.

The people stood on the rocks gaping with sheer amazement, watching the boats go through. Certainly we were the first to attempt this water. By using the loud-hailer I think we were able to convince the people of our potential power! The fish team laid gill nets tonight. Chimpanzees were heard in the forest.

Medical: Corporal Sanders is still suffering badly from his malaria and I realize that we must evacuate him as soon as possible. It may be necessary to get him out from the nearest point which a vehicle can reach. Looking ahead, I think this must be at Wanie Rukula and I have alerted FST/C. Serious casualties are always a danger on such an expedition where it is difficult to get an aircraft near the river.

The Panasonic radios are invaluable although it is very difficult to hear what is being said above the roar of the river. During our emergency today I received a message from the recce group commander, 'Recce 2 power gone, taking in water'. Unable to hear clearly above the noise, I thought for one awful moment that he had said, 'Powell gone'. I was thankful to discover afterwards that Bob Powell was in fact safe.

Checked damage to boats from today's incident. Only one engine is in bad order. Weather getting noticeably hotter as we approach the equator. Natives along the banks regard us with slightly less enthusiasm than those earlier.

Friday 29 November

Night postion: 00°00·7'N, 25°30·3'E. Distance run: 45 km. There were no rapids and we crossed the equator at noon. Temperature was 42° Centigrade in the sun. A small ceremony was held to mark the occasion. The banks are covered in dense jungle with a few limestone outcrops. Wild lemons were plentiful.

Zoology: excellent fish samples were found in the village below the rapids, plus many mormyrids not usually found in the rapids and a species of these mormyrids were found to be very large with no gill parasites found on these rapids fish. Some new fish samples also found. The last five days spent in looking for fossil fish in the limestone outcrop nearby have produced fifty specimens all about one inch long and sardine-like, about one hundred million years old.

Entomology: large caterpillars, ants, large flies (one inch long), bees and land crabs seen.

Medical: many umbilical hernias seen amongst local people in the villages, plus one acondronplastic dwarf who came as a guide.

Geology: it is of interest that the oolitic limestone here shows that the area was once marine. Theory also proved by fish fossils. One cave found with reputed initials of H. M. Stanley in it, but on close inspection nothing definite could be found. A large limestone kiln was situated at the riverside. It had been in use since 1959 and is still being worked today.

Radio getting very difficult and some confusion in orders occurring because we cannot get messages through clearly.

Have been looking for evidence of a large river coming in from west, for I notice on Stanley's map that he marked the Wakuti which he also said might be the Luamami. I believe this is a confusion with the river we call the Lomami which in fact runs parallel to the Zaire and further to the west. I cannot see how he thought that such a large river was coming in at this point.

Stanley's passage in these parts was greatly interrupted by the attacks of the hostile Baswa, and he fought many battles at the cataracts which we have just come down. This area provided the ideal opportunity for the natives to ambush him, for he had to cut a track about a kilometre and a half long and seven metres wide through the jungle to circumnavigate the worst of the falls. I can imagine the effort required, particuarly with a hostile crowd opposing you. Stanley talks of people being armed with bows and arrows and I have seen people so armed in the last few days. However, I do not now think there is any real cause for concern and the people I have appointed to keep a sharp eye open for any sign of trouble are equally happy. Nevertheless our LOs are uneasy. Our guns are ready for use in case of trouble. Stanley wrote:

January 4th: While engaged in making several coils of rope out of the lianes or convolvuli we were disturbed again by the Baswa who were again repelled, while each successful shot was responded to with wild cries of surprise, rage, and sorrow mixed. A small party was sent to survey the right bank below, but the whole force of the river almost rushed with intense impetuosity against the right bank which formed a deep bend, barring all possibility of proceeding by right branch and numerous wrecks of canoes strewed along shore testified to the destructive force of the waters. I then manned 2 double canoes and crossed above the Rapids to the left bank along which ran a small stream though deep and but little disturbed, which presently broke into numerous foamy streams among rocky islands covered with mangrove, others with palms, bananas, and fields of the fierce Baswa tribe. One small branch still continued its quiet flow but presently this fell also rapidly over sheets of dark brown rock.

January 5th: Crossed over to the left bank and descended by the left branch and camped near its Falls. Having discovered that to float the canoes down the falls was impossible, I sent the men to work to cut a road 20 feet wide through the dense jungle. A mile in length was found sufficient to take us below the Falls to where the stream renewed its quiet flow. Within this mile there are two falls of about 4 feet and two steep rapids down which the water rushes with terrible force. Owing to the severe punishment given to the Baswa 2 days previously, we were not disturbed today at our work. Tomorrow we hope to begin dragging the canoes overland below the Falls.

January 6th: Commenced the work of hauling the canoes by land below the Falls. By noon we had carried the boat, dragged seven canoes. Furious rain had then set in which put a stop to the work. Our force is now divided a half below the Falls and half above. The Baswa having been quieted have abandoned the attempt to molest us.

January 7th: This morning continued our labours and by noon we were all embarked in our canoes and afloat once more. Descended cautiously about 4 miles along the left bank, and landed at Cheandoah Island of the Baswa tribe who had challenged us to war. Landed a force and captured the Island after three shots! The suddenness of our arrival had completely upset their calculations and their spirit. We captured about 30 goats and an abundance of food, bananas, chickens, eggs with an immense amount of native African booty consisting of spears, knives, shields, iron wire etc.. We also captured a woman and a child to whom we were indebted for names of places and other local information, amongst which we heard of a terrible tribe called the Bakumu Cannibals who make a clean sweep of tribes such as the Wavinza, Mwana-Ntaba and Baswa. They are armed with bows and arrows. We are told also that they have heard of us and mean to see of what stuff we are made.

January 8th: Halt at Cheandoah Island.

Explored island, found it defended on each side by terrible Falls and Rapids. Explored right bank found no road, then crossed over to left bank which to our minds seemed easier. Captured a man today who has repaid us with lies. He was perfectly unintelligible to all our interpreters.

West of the Island, Cheandoah presents a picture of the force of a large river descending a steep slope. Enormous whirlpools with the centre about 18 ins below the edge. We pushed an empty canoe into the influence of one, saw it whirl round, drawn in and shot up again stern foremost. Another singular scene I witnessed:

in the neighbourhood of the Rapids are circular basins of rock and still streamlike reaches of water, which every now and then are strongly agitated, rise nearly a foot immediately and as quickly subside.

January 9th: Left Cheandoah Island and crossed over to left bank. As we were exploring a creek that seemed to follow a course of the river, we were surprised to see a large crowd of natives in war paint and with shields. No work could be done in the jungle, such as road-making, with camps undefended, if they were permitted to overawe the working party or to wound one single man. These were the terrible Bakumu, who had made mincemeat of so many tribes, and who have promised to try our mettle. The boat came out of the creek and a single shot cleared the banks while loud cries of women and shouts of men testified to its success. We then landed and guided by the cries followed them, and came to two villages strongly defended by heaped brushwood and prostrated trees, where we found the people prepared for a fight. Charging through the bush we entered the first village and drove them flying into the woods with a loss of five or six more. About 60 shields and 100 spears were found thrown away by the fugitives. We then set fire to the villages and retraced our steps to begin the work of cutting out a road, and hauling in the canoes overland. By night we had cut our road, dragged all our canoes on land . . .

January 10th: Completed the work of hauling the canoes from Bukumu villages on left bank to river north of Cheandoah and opposite Ntunduru Island. Made our camp on a small island protected by a fosse-like stream, and cut a road 1½ miles long to tomorrow's camp.

January 11th: Floated the canoes down two miles of stream and Rapids to camp opposite north end of Ntunduru Island. It has been a terribly trying day. Six canoes were floated down safely enough early in the morning. The seventh canoe was taken by Muscati, Uledi Muscati and Zaidi, one of my Captains. Muscati, the steersman, did not understand his work and soon upset his canoe in a piece of bad rapids which soon smashed it to pieces. Muscati and Uledi managed to swim to Ntunduru where they were shortly after saved by the Chief Captain Manwa Sera, but poor Zaidi . . . found himself perched in the centre of the Falls, with about 50 yards of falling water and furious black-brown waves on either side of him.

Called to the scene, I could scarcely believe my eyes or realise what strange chance had placed him there, and a more aweful scene I could hardly believe few men had witnessed than I did. The solitary man seated on the pointed rock with the brown waves rising to his knees seemed to be much calmer than any of us who gazed upon him in his terrible position. We then cast about for means to save him. We first lashed several lengths of creepers to a canoe and lowered it down to him, but the instant it seemed to reach him, the force of the running water was so great that the stout creeper snapped like pack thread and the canoe swept by like an arrow, and was engulfed. Then we tried to toss sticks, stools – wooden – into the middle of the stream, but everything was swept away and still the silent man sat witnessing our repeated efforts and we felt each moment that his doom was certain though protracted.

Then I called for another canoe and to this I lashed an inch rope – tent rope – and two stout creepers each 70 yards long and got two volunteers to enter the canoe and paddle it to mid-stream, which of itself was hard work. Five times this method failed to reach him; the sixth time getting more emboldened as the rope and creepers proved strong, we managed to touch his arm, but the current swept it away immediately. The seventh time Zaidi was struck by the creeper thrown to him and instantly fell like a shot into the gulf below. Thirty seconds passed and as no signs of him were seen, we feared he was lost and began to look for his struggling form in the waves below, when his head rose slowly above the water. 'Pull away,' I shouted, tent rope and the two creepers parted, and the canoe began to move down the opposite fall, but Zaidi acting like an anchor caused the canoe to veer to an island below the Fall and all three working as desperate men can work managed to bring the canoe to the island all safe. Though we hurrahed with relieved hearts, their position was still but a reprieve from death. A Fall 50 yards in width separated the island from us, and to the right was a fall about 300 yards wide, and below them was half a mile of Falls and Rapids and great whirlpools and waves rising like hills in the middle of the terrible stream, and below these were the cannibals of Wane-Mukwa. How to reach the island was the question which now perplexed us. We tied a stone to about 60 yards of whipcord and after about the 50th effort they managed to catch it. To the end of the whipcord they tied the tent rope, which had parted before, and drawing it to our side, tied it to three stout creepers, which they drew across and fastened to a rock, by which we thought we had bridged the stream. 'Now the boldest of you pull yourself across.' We heard them debating as to who should go first. Then Uledi, one of the volunteers, shouting: 'In the name of God,' climbed gallantly into the stream, but alas he had made but two pulls when the faithless convolvuli broke and he was compelled to pull back to the island, where as night had now fallen we left them after many encouragements and returned to our camps.

Meantime, the eighth canoe, whose steersman was the coxswain of the *Lady Alice* had likewise got upset, and the coxswain out of six who were upset was drowned to my great regret as my boat-people were the most select out of the Expedition for smartness, civility, bravery and every other quality which endears a follower to a Commander. Heavens! An awful day altogether, not very unlike January 12th, 1876.

January 12th: My first duty this morning was to send greetings to my three brave boys on the Island in the Falls and to send assurances that preparations were being made for their deliverance. I sent a party of 30 men to search for strong cane and another to make communications again with whipcord with the island. About 9 a.m. abundance of 2 inch cane, 1 inch and $\frac{1}{2}$ inch were brought with which we prepared three lines, each sufficient to sustain three men in the water, but to make assurance and success trebly sure, we succeeded in sending three lines across to the island which they fastened to the rocky points. Then hailing them, I asked them if they were sure they could haul themselves across; if not, I would send each man a separate line, to tie round his waist. They shouted a reply that if I was sure the lines would not break, they could; to which I answered that they would haul a ship across. Then Uledi lifted his hands up, muttered a short prayer and laughingly leapt in, catching hold of the cables as he fell into the depths of the Falls. Soon he rose, hauling himself hand over hand, the waves brushing his face and rising over his head, until it seemed as if he could never find time to breathe, but by jerking his body upward occasionally with a desperate effort, he so managed as to survive the waves and to haul himself across near to us, where a score of hands stood ready to snatch the half smothered man. Zaidi next followed but, after the tremendous proof he gave of his courage and deliberately tenacious hold, not much fear was entertained for him and he came safe to be congratulated for his double escape from death.

The rescue of Zaidi

Marzouk, the youngest, was the last and we held our very breaths while the gallant boy struggled with a terrible rush of water. In the middle of raising himself to breathe, he let go of two lines and barely caught hold of the third, and our anxiety was intense for a few seconds lest he should despair and relax his hold; and to prevent this I shouted out harshly: 'Pull away, you fool. Be a man.' At which with three strokes he pulled himself within reach of our willing hands to be hugged and fondled by all. The cheers we gave were heard far above the roar of the waters, and the camp heard it and knew that the three most gallant lads of the Expedition had been saved.

When we had collected ourselves a little, we set to work to begin cutting the road one and a half miles long to pass this terrible scene altogether by land.

At the north end of Ntunduru, four separate streams unite in so many Falls and Rapids and then the limited waters gather themselves into one huge boiling cauldron, and a mound-like body of water, and hurls itself down several feet with tremendous uproar just south of Asama Island. The distance is barely ¾ mile but it is one of the wildest sights of raging waters, brown waves, etc conceivable . . .

So Stanley battled his way northward along the mighty river. The lesson he had taught the savage Bakumu meant that he was left unmolested as he advanced, pausing on 17 January 1877 to investigate the limestone caves near what is now called Songa.

Saturday 30 November

We remained at Songa for the day. Corporal Brian Sanders was at last evacuated by Major Bill Coleridge who had come down by vehicle from Kisangani and reached the river on the far side.

Zoology: the fish section was working in forest streams collecting by nets and on one or two occasions helped by the sappers with a little TNT. Seven species of fish, all most interesting, were collected including one Barbus, which may be a new species for this area. Another twelve fish fossils were collected and many scales were noted to be fossilized in the rock. Professor Geoffrey Haselwood continued his collection of bile from the fish. The only other animal seen was one black and white monkey which might have been a colobus.

Medical: more umbilical hernias noted.

For some days we have been listening to the thud, thud of the talking drums on the river banks around us. These are used to pass messages from one village to another. One outpost drum is established near the limekiln, and in an effort to find out if the natives had seen any of the lost camera boxes I asked if a message could be passed by drum. Apparently the small drum is not powerful enough for this, and we therefore went to see the big one up in Songa village.

War-drums seen by Stanley

Walking up past Dr Alan Bartram and his fish fossil collecting party, we passed through a grove of rubber trees and eventually came to a ruined plantation. The village now encompasses part of the old plantation buildings and beneath a thatched shelter stood the great drum. The drummer gave a demonstration and claimed that he could transmit a message for thirty kilometres by day and fifty by night. He relayed the messages in phrases or groups of words. I gave him the message and for some ten minutes he thundered away at his work. I noticed that the drumsticks were of hardwood wrapped in latex, almost identical to those seen by Stanley on his travels. After these energies I gave the drummer fifty makutas (approximately 50p) as payment, for which he seemed very grateful, and we then took photographs and film of him at work. It will be interesting to see if anything results.

We tried an interesting experiment with one of the giant craft and fitted *Barclays Bank* with a sail which did give her a very slow velocity downstream. Her skipper, Major Billy Bowles, is something of a yachtsman and this was his idea! One of the Avon S400s has had its hull ripped and is being repaired. The damage to the boats is really very minimal and quite surprising considering the conditions that we are going through. The Avons are remarkably tough and every bit as good as they were on the Blue Nile. This evening Mr and Mrs John Strugnal, from the Bralima brewery in Kisangani, came up river with fifteen crates of beer. They stayed the night with us and we had a very good party in the area of the limekilns.

Sunday 1 December

The fleet moved forward towards Kisangani. We met FST/C on the east bank at Wanie-Rukula. Following this we crossed a series of shallow rapids approximately three kilometres to the north. With the river rising there were no great problems although I could see these must have been an obstacle to Stanley. Lunch was taken on the west bank as we approached the seventh and final cataract of the Stanley Falls. I had gone ahead with the recce section to examine the falls in detail, but of course my FST parties had already looked at them and Bill Coleridge had already taken one small Avon boat down the main chute with safety. The falls, although they look most impressive, are only about 170 metres across. The river itself being approximately four hundred metres wide at this point, narrows to pour over the falls. The drop cannot be much more than three metres at the most and the waves at the bottom about one and a half metres high. There is only one fall itself and there is smooth water on both sides. I had no hesitation in ordering the fleet to take the chute on the east side of the falls and we formed up in convoy to do it in style. While lunching amongst the bamboo groves on the west bank, I saw evidence of the proposed canal that the Belgians had intended to build before independence. Concrete markers were in the ground.

Whilst we formed up, the recce party discovered that we had actually approached the falls on the wrong side of the long island and that there was some danger that we might be swept into fish traps, erected by the Wagenia tribe. Being Sunday, great crowds had gathered to watch us cross the falls and we did this with the Beaver overhead at exactly 1500 hours in the following order: Recce 1; *La Vision*; the Avon 650; *Barclays Bank*; Recce 2; *David Gestetner*. The recce boats and the Avon 650 were flung high into the air as they crossed the waves. The giant boats made a very smooth passage but *David Gestetner* demolished the fish trap *en route*. Thousands of people cheered ecstatically at the show, and a grand party awaited us on shore through the kindness of the Bralima brewery who also provided a very welcome dinner for the crew of *La Vision* at a local hotel. Meanwhile Derek Jackson and his support group were flying in by DC 4 from Kindu. The fleet and all our stores are billeted in a vast Bralima warehouse by the river.

Stanley shooting the rapids

It was late January 1877 when Stanley reached the seventh cataract.

January 26th: Descended one mile to the Wenya Falls and cut a road across a neck of land beyond which is the Wenya Creek on the right bank . . . Fall is about 10 feet but there is a great slope and as the river narrows to about 500 yards, the force of the current is terrific, as it rushes through the narrows to the grand breadth below Wenya Island.

These Wenya are cunning and skilful people in some things, but their villages are untidy. They are clever at wooden boxes, paddles, cord making.

Ivory seems to be a drug with them. Three large tusks I found to be perfectly rotten in the villages. They seem to have no use for it after cutting off a foot off the point for the purpose of making war-horns and pestles to pound corn.

They catch an enormous amount of fish by means of poles and conical baskets attached to long canes.

January 27th: Descended over 200 yards on rocks by a system of railway sleepers topped with rollers, and then 2 miles of a series of waterfalls and rapids which this creek makes until it approaches the north end of Wenya Island, when it becomes still and sluggish.

Seventh cataract, Stanley Falls

The Wenya planned to attack us by two points, one from the north end of Wenya Island ascending up-creek and the other by striking right across River to take us in rear while our working parties were scattered over the length of two miles dragging heavy canoes over the rock terraces. Thirteen guns and a few successful well placed shots sent them flying to the village at the point opposite Wenya Island on the right bank.

January 29th: Voyage continues from Usimbi to Erere Island.

So Stanley had reached the future site of the city named after him – Stanleyville (now called Kisangani).

Monday 2 December

And so, in four days we have negotiated the Stanley Falls which took the famous explorer some twenty-three days to move through and around, almost a hundred years ago. The success is undoubtedly due to the very thorough reconnaissance facilitated by the technology of the twentieth century; especially the video equipment, Polaroid cameras and, of course, the inflatable boats. Nevertheless, it would be wrong to think that it has been too easy, and we very nearly had a bad accident at Ubundu. I consider that our display of force in the last month may well have prevented any rebels from attacking us. Now I believe that the risk is reduced but nevertheless one cannot afford to be complacent.

Now we have to think ahead. Between here and Kinshasa, the capital, there is over 1000 kilometres of wide trouble-free water. There may be problems, but I believe the major difficulty will be keeping people from getting bored to tears with this long journey. I propose to move off and see the scientists who are operating on the flank, and also to go in search of the rare okapi. We shall probably leave a large party in Kisangani to continue scientific work while the fleet pushes on to the west and the Atlantic. Meanwhile I intend to send an overland party south and west from

Kisangani, through Kananga and on to Kinshasa. This group can link up with the medical research team and give assistance *en route*. The expedition, which I have been able to hold together in a reasonably tight group several hundred kilometres wide, is now about to spread out to something like one part being in London, with another group in Greece and another in Sicily. That is if you work in straight lines and assume the extremities of the expedition that will be reached by the time this adventure is over. The logistic problems are frightening but I have every confidence in Derek Jackson and his group who have already achieved miracles. Our problem is that with very little money and not much likelihood of any more coming from England, we have to do everything on a shoestring. I can imagine what Napoleon felt like before Moscow; the only difference is that we still seem to be winning!

The Engineers and FST/B arrived in Kisangani after a slightly dramatic journey from Kindu. They had passed through an area which was certainly hostile to the government, and even the LOs had been greatly worried. But with their usual dash and tenacity, the team had got through in spite of breakdowns and having to build bridges. *En route* they passed the relics of the mercenary wars, including burnt-out tanks. They had quite a story to tell and it was a fine achievement for them to get through so quickly.

The brewery very kindly gave us a fine party this afternoon where we met General Mena, a former military attaché in London. He had been there in 1965, was very pro-British, and offered to help us in any way he could. He is now the army commander of the region, based at Kisangani.

The hospitality being accorded to us in this city is enormous, both from the Zairois and the Europeans. It is certainly a good feeling to be welcome, and everyone is congratulating us on having navigated both the Gates of Hell and the Stanley Falls. Our own members are beginning to think that the whole thing is just a little too easy, an illusion

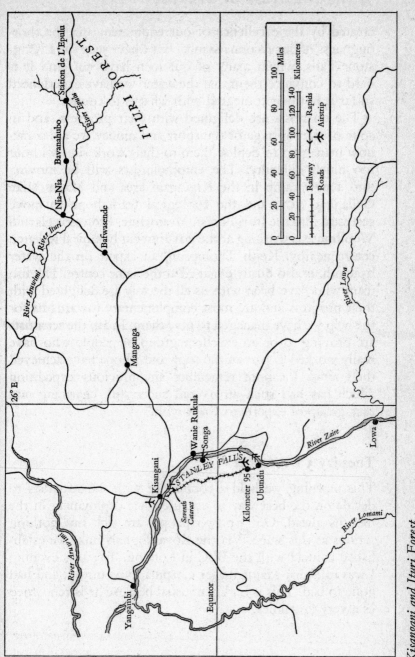

Kisangani and Ituri Forest

created by the excellence of our equipment and the thoroughness of our reconnaissance. But I have seen the Livingstone Falls, which many of our men have not, and it is hard to convince them that the water we have experienced so far is nothing compared with what is to come.

The scientists are delighted with their progress, and in spite of the shortage of transport and money we are somehow managing to deploy them to their work sites without too much difficulty. The entomologists will be moving into a new camp in the Kisangani area and Major Mike Gallagher, RCT, and the zoological team hope to move eastward into the Ituri Forest. Meanwhile, Professor Harold Woolhouse is working at the government botanical research centre nearby. Keith Thompson, an expert on the water hyacinth, is also busily engaged at the same centre. The fish team who have been with us all the way are delighted with their progress and are most complimentary towards us for the help we have managed to give them. In all, the scientists are proving to be an excellent group of people who have really worked as part of the team and I hope have achieved their aims. I cannot remember any previous expedition which has had such an overall successful, charming and easy group of experts to work with.

Tuesday 3 December

This morning we held a conference with the scientists to decide on the best way to execute their deployment in the months ahead. One or two people are sick but nothing serious at this stage. Via the Royal Signals link, we established contact with the BBC in London. Towards evening I was told that Major Roger Chapman was unwell and had gone to bed. This is highly unusual because he is renowned as a very fit soldier.

Wednesday 4 December

His Excellency the British Ambassador and the Defence Attaché arrived by air from Kinshasa at 1125 hours. They are to be with us for a few days to see the expedition and meet local officials. Meanwhile, plans for the okapi hunt are being finalized. Strangely, it seems to be a sensitive area for us to visit and not quite so simple to get permission to go there as I had first thought.

Scientists are now starting to deploy in our very battered and tired old Land-Rovers. My only concern is that these vehicles will last. Already one has had to be written off and another is in almost the same condition. The transport problems are growing daily.

Excellent dinner with ambassador and local officials in Zaire Palace Hotel tonight.

Thursday 5 December

His Excellency went out with the fleet this morning and accompanied them for a few kilometres on their way down-river. I conferred with him at Tac HQ in the afternoon and discussed some of our problems. At the same time, I was able to report that we are on schedule and that our morale is very high.

Roger Chapman was taken to hospital this afternoon with peritonitis and an operation was later performed by John Chapman-Smith and Viv Jones. His condition is only average and already there are grounds for concern. Apparently Roger was operated on with only a spinal anaesthetic. He still joked about an eye surgeon and a gynaecologist combining to cut him open!

Ambassador and party returned to Kinshasa by air this afternoon. With them went Captain Tom Mabe who is to join FST/A on the jet boat operation and also Captain Paul Turner who is to act as an LO in Kinshasa. FST/C departed to go overland via Kananga to Kinshasa. Chimp Force came in, having done an excellent job although they did not find the pygmy chimpanzee. Gordon Mitchell, our tireless quartermaster, has now set up his new empire in the brewery warehouse and is dispensing stores in his usual efficient manner. One of two items of equipment are in fact letting us down. I was particularly concerned to note that the Speedlines (rocket-carried life-lines) are not standing up to the rough wear and tear of the expedition. The lids on the plastic containers keep coming off, lines fall out and tangle, and one rocket we tried failed to ignite. This is a serious problem as we may well need them in the future. Our lives could depend on these rockets.

Friday 6 December

During the night Roger Chapman's condition deteriorated rapidly. The medical officers reported to me shortly after dawn to say that his chance of survival was only fifty-fifty. While I was in conference with General Mena, Derek Jackson burst in so suddenly that the sentry outside fired a shot in the air to stop him! Derek had sensed the situation was getting grave and came with an urgent request for the general to commandeer a civilian DC4 to arrange immediate evacuation by air. Our Beaver's compass is out of action, and anyway the chances of a patient's survival during travel in a light aircraft for that distance would be slim. During the morning Roger's condition continued to deteriorate. A grim-faced little group stood outside the local hospital ward while our doctors and nurses fought for his life.

Eventually we were able to load Roger and Dr Viv Jones, plus Pam Baker as the nurse, on to the DC 4, which took of for Kinshasa at approximately 1200 hours. Roger is a great friend to many of us and we are all praying hard that he will survive this severe illness. The problem is that with no laboratory facilities here, it is difficult to ascertain just exactly what is wrong with him. However, the local hospital authorities and their Egyptian doctor have been most kind and they have done everything possible to assist. It is fortunate that we have Pam with us. She has worked in the clinic at Kinshasa and knows the medical set-up there and the people concerned. By sending her with Roger I feel happy that he will get the very best attention. It is incidents like this that makes one really appreciate the value of the girls on this journey.

The reconnaissance of the Livingstone Falls by jet should be starting now. I am concerned for the people involved as the waters there are especially dangerous. Very few of us on the expedition really understand the full capabilities of the jet craft, but they have the inventor's son in charge of the party and I am sure they have got the best crew possible.

Our fleet has now covered 3200 kilometres. Mike Gambier, who is once again in command of the boats, reports that morale is high but mosquitoes are very bad at night. Communication with him is still poor. The river is now more than three kilometres wide and flowing at 4·3 km per hour. It is covered with a mass of islands so that it is difficult to see across from one bank to the other. One of the reconnaissance boats was holed by a log but is being repaired.

Saturday 7 December

Scientists continue to deploy and preparations go ahead for okapi hunt. I have had to postpone departure for this due to lack of information on the animals, but Valerie Jones is working hard arranging the visit and we hope to leave shortly.

The situation on Roger Chapman is more encouraging. Apparently he is making reasonable progress in hospital in Kinshasa. Before leaving to look for the okapi I must await the return of the TV team with whom communication is not easy at present, as they are with the botanists to the west of Kisangani. If they have not returned by tomorrow

I must press forward, otherwise there will be insufficient time for our task.

The fleet appears to be sailing on with no great problems. Mike Gambier reports by radio that they have entered the tribal area of the Mongo. (President Mobutu is said to be a member of this tribe.)

Sunday 8 December

Moved off with Tac HQ in two Land-Rovers taking with me *Daily Telegraph* team, Doug Newby (photographer) and Sergeant Malcolm Pace as fitter. Corporal Sam Qarau went with us as signaller. We left at 1015 hours for Station de l'Epulu. The road was very good and straight, hard-packed red earth through dense jungle. Occasional pot-holes were hazardous particularly at speed, as vehicle I was driving had no brakes and poor steering! As we neared end of our four hundred kilometre journey we met up in the darkness with otter-shrew collecting party who with Sergeant-Major McGee are working in forest in this area. They had arrived previous day and were in good heart. Zoologist Dr Ken Joysey was very enthusiastic about the area and hopes to catch at least one otter-shrew alive. Major Mike Gallagher was with them doing good work collecting bats, snakes and other beasts of the forest for the British Museum (Natural History). They had already established close liaison with pygmies and had some interesting souvenirs to show. Reached government guest house at Station de l'Epulu at approximately midnight. There, with help of letter written by General Mena, we were made very welcome and given comfortable beds for the night. On the way we had stopped at a small village 'pub' for meal. A man appeared to serve us wearing spectacles with no glass in them. When asked why this was he replied, 'Because the glass is too expensive.'

Back on the river, the fleet report that the water hyacinth

Left: Okapi bull near Epulu

Below: J. B-S with young fish-eating crocodile

Opposite top: David Gestetner
sets out to tackle Kinsuka.
Lt John Watkin on the helm,
Cpl Sam Qarau sits by him
with the National Panasonic
radio

Opposite centre: David Gestetner
at the moment of impact
with the rock ledge that
smashed her engine upwards

Opposite below: Portaging
La Vision at Yalala

Right: The Edwin Arnold
Falls with Jet 2 in fore-
ground. Ralph Brown at the
wheel

Below: Jon Hamilton takes
Jet 1 through a moderate
rapid

Left: Barclays Bank heads out into the Atlantic at the end of the expedition

Centre: At the Presidency. *L to r:* J. B-S, Richard Snailham, Capt Kayalo (glasses), and President Mobutu Seso Seko

Below: Thanksgiving service at sunset on Sunday, 19 January – on Atlantic

has become established along the river bank, but has not as yet started growing in the soil. The river banks are swampy, riddled with mosquitoes and largely devoid of humans, save where the ground is firm enough to support a village. The few villages seen are hemmed in by thick impenetrable rain forests and look as though they are just about to be pushed into the river by the jungle.

Mike Gambier says that all along this stretch there are huge flies with large green eyes. They arrive on the boats in swarms and have bites like crocodiles! They appear to inhabit the clumps of water hyacinth. Communications with fleet very difficult.

Monday 9 December

During night Peter Marett arrived with a second Land-Rover, having waited for the TV team, but because of camera problems they were unable to come. I was slightly put out because whole operation had been arranged for their benefit. At Station de l'Epulu we were shown two fine bull okapis, which were very tame. Apparently a further seventeen had died of some unknown disease a few months before. The research station seems to be well run and the conservator was enthusiastic about his programme. We photographed extensively and also saw four types of antelope and two chimpanzees, plus other small unidentified monkeys that were being kept in the research centre. The guest house in which we stayed was clean and pleasant and the conservator refused to charge us as he said we were guests of the government. This was thanks to the letters from General Mena and a Belgian wild-life expert, Monsieur Pierret. The hotel opposite the guest house had been burned down during Jacques Schramme's operations with the mercenaries. A Bailey bridge, about one hundred metres in length, now crosses the river and was erected by the Royal Engineers after the troubles. We passed over many such bridges on the way from Kisangani. The road which we had travelled along was that used by the mercenaries in their withdrawal to the east. Many of the bridges were of a triple-double structure with reinforcing that appeared to be in need of maintenance. The bridges were built across existing piers of the old bridges.

The research into the okapi seems to be efficient and sincerely undertaken. Learning that okapi were captured in the forest not far away I sought the co-operation of the conservator to arrange an immediate visit to the area. He told me that the area most favoured was some fifteen kilometres south of Bavanahubo, which was approximately eighty kilometres west of Epulu. Therefore after lunch we drove to the village, stopping *en route* to buy spears, bows and arrows and impliments from the many pygmy villages alongside the route. At Bavanahubo we found the village chief whose name was Mayla. A most helpful man who provided a hut for us to camp in for the night.

On the evening radio schedule we learned of the continued improvement of Roger Chapman. Apparently the tubes which had been inserted down his nose and into his stomach had been removed. Pam Baker is nursing him at night and he is making reasonable progress.

FST/C reported that Sergeant Kuba (LO) had been arrested by the local commissaire during their drive towards Kananga. Apparently it was now all right and only a misunderstanding. In the pygmy village we sat around the fire and made our plans with local hunters to seek the okapi with our cameras, starting at dawn. The pygmies seem to be very peaceful and were extremely hospitable. They are apparently not very numerous but nevertheless staunchly maintain their traditional way of life. Their livelihood is mainly obtained from hunting and the gathering of fruits and berries in the Ituri Forest. This dense jungle is not unlike that of Darien and one can imagine the problems that Stanley had on the Emin Pasha Expedition of 1886–89 when he had to force the passage all the way to the Nile through this same dense forest.

In their strange warbling voices the little pygmies told us many tales of the forest. They explained that only chiefs were allowed to sit on the skin of the okapi, the reason being that this is supposed to bring the chief 'plenty of pretty girls'.

Mike Gambier reports fleet has reached Bumba where it is to collect fuel. They were well entertained by local mission schools, and met up with the Beaver which brought them mail and also Nurse Adrianne Damgaard who is to join the fleet. Thanks to the research done prior to this trip by Squadron Leader Mike Barnard, the navigation is not proving too much of a problem in spite of the many confusing islands.

Tuesday 10 December

The okapi hunt moved off at first light leaving Sergeant Pace and Corporal Qarau at our base in the village. We took with us six pygmies and some other local Zairois. They were armed with short bows and arrows approximately thirty-six centimetres long. The arrows were either tipped with thin metal heads or simply sharpened to a point on the wood, which was then burned to give it extra hardness. It was explained to me that the poison which they extract from a certain berry, is used only on the wooden tips. The pygmies make small serrations on the edge to hold the poison. It is only necessary to prick the target slightly, for once blood is drawn and the poison goes into the system, paralysis and death is reported to follow very quickly. They also carry short spears but these are mainly for self-defence. Our LO, Lieutenant Bongo, interpreted for us through a Lingala-speaking Zairois who in turn spoke to the pygmies. They were jolly fellows who could move very rapidly by passing underneath the dense vegetation. We, being taller, had great difficulty and were soon puffing and panting as we followed them. One of the pygmies accidentally shot himself in the foot with an arrow and, although he sustained a nasty wound, happily went on walking for the rest of the day.

Initially we followed an overgrown track which the pygmies said they had made to enable them to take in government officials to track down okapi once a year. They described to me the method of catching the beast. This is to dig a pit approximately two metres deep and cover it with brushwood and leaves. When the animal falls in, the pygmies gradually fill the pit with earth, thus allowing the okapi to tread its way upwards. When it is almost at ground level they seize and bind it and transport it back to the village where it is handed over to the Conservation Department. Apparently there is one big hunt each year. The okapi is peculiar to Zaire and is a rare animal by any accounts. I felt we should be really fortunate if we did in fact manage to see one.

By 1100 hours we had marched fifteen and a half kilometres (according to Peter Marett's reckoning). The tracks and footpaths were quite reasonable but without the pygmies we should have been hopelessly lost. We frequently saw okapi spoor, and several times came close to them, but in the dense vegetation it was impossible to see more than twenty metres. There was much evidence of elephant and occasionally we heard them crashing about ahead of us, freshly dropped dung still steaming on some of the paths. Numerous monkeys and one or two snakes, and a number of birds in the trees. The jungle was almost entirely secondary and movement extremely difficult off the tracks. The area obviously held much large forest game although seeing it was going to be difficult. We had lunch at an old hunting camp, and then split into three parties to increase our chances of spotting an okapi and made our way in an extended line back towards the road. On the way many monkeys were seen and one party – including myself, Valerie Jones and Lieutenant Bongo – bumped into a small party of forest-type elephant (the pygmy or dwarf variety). Without warning four of the beasts charged and missed us by only fifteen metres. I noticed they were much smaller than the elephants I had seen previously, probably only about two metres at the shoulder. They bypassed us and carried on down the valley towards the stream making a most fearful din. Valerie and I followed for a short while, hoping to be able to photograph them, but they soon left us behind. Eventually we reached the road at approximately 1500 hours, having covered nearly seventeen miles.

The pygmies gave us a great welcome, having come up from the village with Corporal Qarau in one of the Land-Rovers. They sang hunting songs and escorted us back to our hut. At the village we met a group of young English people travelling to Nairobi with an overland travel firm. They were apparently behind schedule, but seemed to be enjoying themselves travelling in open ex-Army four-ton trucks with old coach seats installed for comfort. The men appeared to be somewhat unkempt, but the girls seemed very pleasant and the whole party was in good spirits. Further down the road we had previously seen a large bus belonging to another company which had broken down and was already a month behind schedule. These parties are typical of the many tours that set out from Britain to take people of all ages on adventure holidays in Africa.

By radio we heard tonight that Sergeant Mick Hough has been evacuated by air to Kinshasa because of complications following his fall from the tree at Kindu. Brain haemorrhage and a split liver are suspected.

Most enjoyable evening spent in being entertained by villagers and pygmies who sang and danced round our camp fire. We in turn provided a few items of entertainment for them which culminated in Valerie doing a Highland sword dance and Sam Qarau spitting flaming paraffin from his mouth. This terrified the pygmies who fled into the night.

The news on the radio was pretty gloomy, logistics still a grave problem. The fleet have now reached Lisala. This is the Zaire River's most northerly point. They report that mosquitoes are the worst they have experienced so far. One hundred counted on a square foot of mesh! Sleep almost impossible. A British Baptist mission secondary school has been very kind to the fleet. Maggie Bush has apparently been trying her hand at navigating; her success marred by the loss of her contact lenses!

Wednesday 11 December

We moved out from pygmy village saying fond farewell at 0730 hours, stopping for a short time at scientists' camp where we saw the holiday firm's bus still unserviceable! The scientists have seen otter-shrews and other animals in the area. They believe the shrews were of the pygmy variety. They are now offering rewards to any hunter who can catch one and hope to get a live specimen. I examined the zoologists' textbooks and confirmed that the elephants we saw yesterday were of the pygmy variety. A small antelope, which had been knocked down accidentally by Lieutenant Bongo last night, was handed over for examination. Having discussed conditions and deployment with scientists, I decided to deploy more people to this area in the effort to find an otter-shrew alive and will therefore give orders on return to Kisangani. The Gurkhas will be especially suitable for this task.

Heavy rain and thunder during return journey, in spite of dry season! Roads became extremely slippery and at one point we had to stop and move a fallen tree. We arrived back at Kisangani after dark and had a puncture just as we entered town. Many problems on return including difficulties in Kananga. Found that TV team had lost a tape recorder and valuable tapes, stolen from camp. Valerie Jones demonstrated her powers as a cook and produced an excellent evening meal for us.

Heard from Mike Gambier that fleet had been forced to purchase insecticides as mosquitoes had got quite unbearable. He tells me river is now eight kilometres wide and covered in even more clumps of hyacinth, as far as the eye can see. They camped for night at Mobindo and were

treated to much palm wine and a superb display of traditional dancing and singing. Captain Kayalo, our senior LO,
is apparently in good form and becoming quite popular
with the crew. His only worry is about the inability to
communicate with his army headquarters. The main
problem being that even our radios cannot reach Kinshasa.
Apparently Jim Masters got full of palm wine and fell
headlong into the river while trying to spend a penny at
0130 hours!

Thursday 12 December

Logistic support group moved out today by river steamer.
All stores were loaded on board and they will make dumps
as they go down river for fleet to pick up.

Reorganized FST/B and the scientists. The Gurkhas
will now go into the Ituri Forest and work with the pygmies.
This should be most interesting. Transport problems
continue to beset us, and of course local vehicles are far too
costly to hire. If only we had more money, what an expedition this could be. We are none the less very grateful to our
friends in Kisangani who are doing everything they can to
help.

Now expedition has reached half-way point, I can sum-
marize our problems as follows:

Finance. The lack of money has meant that we are short of
transport and therefore deployment is difficult. This means
I cannot use all my personnel effectively. Also some of the
expedition scientists have changed their plans and now tend
to work in larger groups in similar areas, so I have not
needed quite so many administrative personnel to support them as I believed we should when I was still in
England.

Politics. The Zairois continue to be hypersensitive and we
have had to be very careful what we say and do to avoid
causing offence. At Kananga there seems to be a running
problem of the British versus other nationalities in the team.

In minor disagreements, the Zairois side with the Belgians with whom they have a common tongue. Unfortunately, this is too far away for me to be very effective in intervening. I trust to Freddie Rodger's diplomacy to sort this out tactfully.

Personalities. There are no real problems here, perhaps because I am more ruthless. I cannot indeed remember an expedition that has had so few personality problems as this one. The girls are certainly no problem and are working very hard and well. I believe they are a cohesive element in the team.

Mail. The lack and delay of mail is causing worries, but I cannot see that we can do anything to speed it up. Much mail, particularly small parcels, appears to be getting lost. Our lines of communication are really too stretched.

Stores. No real problem except the dire shortage of fuel and Land-Rover spares. Our preparation of the Land-Rovers in Britain was not all that it should have been, particularly the springs which are the weak variety. The Fairey winches that we are using are excellent, however, and have got us out of many a tight corner.

The River. The main reason for success is the thorough reconnaissance we are carrying out and the good equipment that we have; i.e. the boats. The video is especially valuable and I believe we must be the first expedition ever to use this equipment in the field. It is very soldier-proof and stands up to the heat and humidity extremely well. It is under the charge of the signals section. I am most impressed with the way it can be employed easily and quickly, and produce such good results.

Medical. Generally good. So far we have one case of VD, one case of peritonitis, one bad fall, and two cases of chicken-pox. There have been a number of cases of fever and three that are thought to be malaria. We have had some amoebic dysentery, sprains, septic cuts, bites (including one dog bite), some ear trouble, and one or two cases of domestic welfare difficulties back at home. I have reason to suspect that some of our members may be trying out the local drugs, but no British servicemen are involved.

Scientific. No real problems. The scientists are quite wonderful and very understanding. They are by far the best scientists we have ever had with any expedition. They seem to appreciate all our difficulites and indeed the whole problem of logistics in this vast land.

Public Relations. Locally it is very good. Citoyen Mpoy from the Zaire newspaper is an excellent young man who is continuing to write first-class reports. He constantly mentions the good relations between Britain and Zaire! We have been using the films from previous expeditions in the towns to give lectures both for PR purposes and fund-raising.

Discipline. The discipline is fair but I try to avoid the towns if possible. What we really need is an active sergeant-major to look after the number of soldiers. I have noticed that officers tend to be rather hesitant about pulling their soldiers up short on expeditions and I am constantly having to remind them about haircuts and turn-out. The problem is of course that with the scientists bearded and long-haired, it is difficult to keep the soldiers to a normal military type of appearance. There are one or two minor discipline problems with both civilians and soldiers, mostly caused by stupidity and thoughtlessness. Nothing serious.

Weather. The weather really has been pretty good. We seem to have dodged the rain all along the river and yet managed to get just enough water to navigate. I hope that our luck continues to hold out.

Communications. Adequate only. Much of the problem is due to the distance we are now expecting our A14 radios to reach.

Roads. Generally poor and getting worse. The jungle is certainly encroaching on the country's road system.

Rail. In general good and the company, which is nationalized, extremely helpful.

Ferries. Approximately 50 per cent working only.

Air Strips. Many are overgrown, but where they are usuable they are in quite reasonable condition.

Insects. Mosquitoes are bad in places and there are tetse flies and other nuisances, including scorpions.

Animal Hazards. So far only the hippo. Very few crocodile. Snakes numerous.

Internal Air Services. Good, but usually over-booked.

Morale. In general good. This is thanks very often to the free supply of beer; it seems everlasting! Scientists are certainly very happy. I foresee problems with boredom in future and we have already had some signs of this when river parties and others have had to wait for the support group to catch up.

Flew this afternoon with Valerie Jones to Yangambi hoping to see scientists in their camp. We landed at deserted air strip and, in spite of enquiries and previous low flying over villages, could see no scientists. As we taxied to a halt aircraft became surrounded by literally thousands of children who were mildly hostile although I suspect more excited than anything else. We lacked our Polaroid camera which is always a good thing for winning over people's hearts. So instead I made a long speech in very bad French telling them all about the expedition. This only attracted thousands more small children who pressed around us and the aircraft. Cliff Taylor, the pilot, had to keep them from climbing on the plane and doing damage to it. For a short time it seemed we would be overwhelmed by the mob and it was a little unnerving. So I selected largest lad in crowd, put him in charge, and got him to clear a way while we climbed back aboard. As soon as the engines started the children scattered and we took off safely.

On 26th and 27th January 1877 Stanley circumnavigated the final rapids in the difficult stretch he had named the Stanley Falls. His diaries talk of the Wenya, almost certainly the same people who are now called Wagenya. He describes them as cunning and skilful people in some things, but found their villages were untidy. He remarks on their ability for making wooden boxes, paddles and cord, and goes on to say how ivory was a drug to them. He also mentions their use of poles and conical baskets for catching fish, and the 1974 Expedition was to see the very same methods in use today.

Using an improvized railway system Stanley hauled his boats around the last fall and found the river slow flowing, wide and surrounded by extremely hostile natives.

January 29th: Today we have had three fights. Obliged to fight by the savage insolence of men and women. The men generally ranged themselves on the banks with shields and spears, shouting their war cries. To have passed them by in silence would have been to invite further molestation. We at once landed and punished them several times. In the last fight opposite this night's camp Muftah Rufigi of the Mgindo was killed by a desperate savage who attacked him with a knife 18 inches long which cut him on the head, almost severed the right arm from the shoulder, and then buried up to the hilt in his chest.

January 30th: Voyage continues from Erere Island to uninhabited island 6 miles north-west by west from Yangambi.

We were assaulted in the most determined manner by the natives of populous Yangambi. They were in full war paint, and all the medicines and charms were brought forth. They were the bravest we met. Of course, such arrogance met with instant punishment. In an instant we had landed spearmen and musketeers, and in their rear fire was set to the village. We then withdrew to a grassy islet to observe the effect on the natives, lunched, and as they had drawn together on the banks, made a second attempt. But the fire and their losses in dead had quelled their courage. We then proceeded on our way down river, passed two abandoned settlements, the results of former wars . . .

January 31st: Voyage continues from Divari Island.

Today I thought I would try to pass one day without fighting, but just as we left Divari Island we rounded a point where amplest preparations had been made. They had been up all night with drums, building a palisade, making charms, etc. Uganza and Irende opposite had also come up with canoes which they had hidden behind our little island to demonstrate when opportunity offered to our disadvantage. We therefore floated quietly down by them, probably without a shot, had not a mischievous fellow rose and swayed his spear. He was then hushed with one shot, and no more was attempted. We then thought it would be advisable to steer close to the islands and look resolutely away from the natives, but after passing Mawembe some distance, we were followed by six or seven canoes who pulled lustily after us and called out to others hidden behind the small island to advance and eat us. A few harmless shots allayed their rage for our flesh and we came down peacefully to camp on an uninhabited island 17 miles north west of Mawembe.

The utmost vigilance is necessary each night to prevent theft of canoes and night surprises, for the natives are very capable of it. By day, also, for the islands are numerous and communications of alarm and war combinations rapid enough to excite admiration, by means of their enormous wooden drums which are heard at a great distance.

February 1st: Voyage continues from camp on uninhabited island. Today has been another busy day, had three fights, in which the natives must have lost about 30 lives. They first sought to attack us at a market place as we passed by, but we sharply turned round, landed, killed about 10, got an abundance of food and then set fire to the canoes – about 25 in number. At a second market place a similar scene took place. Then proceeded from noon to about 3 pm. We came to Battle River [I assume Stanley was referring to the river at Aruwimi]. Twenty-three canoes came from the left bank. Twenty-one canoes came from Battle River, about 10 of which were enormous things containing probably about 500 men. They advanced to the attack bravely enough with drums and horns and cries. We in the meantime dropped anchor and arranged ourselves in a line across the stream which ran between the mainland and an island at the mouth of Battle River. In a short time we had given them a taste of what they might expect from us, and caused some of the largest to retire wailing. Some of their men were in the river, others lay in the bottom of the canoes groaning and dying. As these retired, a magnificent war canoe came down to reinforce them. It probably was the King's canoe, and contained about 100 men. About 6 were perched on a

Stanley's force repels an attack

platform at the bow, hideously painted and garnished with head-
dresses of feathers, while one stalked backwards and forward
with a crown of feathers. There were probably about 60 paddlers
and each paddle was decorated with an ivory ball handle and the
staff was wound about with copper and iron wire.

So Stanley floated downriver among the maze of islands
and sand-banks. He met varying degrees of hostility, but, as
his reputation of fearsome strength grew, more and more
people began to come to him in peace.

Friday 13 December

The fleet continues to advance down-river at fair speed.
They report cold, overcast and windy weather, but people
are very friendly and entertain them liberally at each stopping place. They are now in the country of the Libinza tribe
who are said to be notorious for their quick, volatile tempers.
So far there has been no trouble.

Communications are growing steadily more difficult as
the boats go farther away. Mike Barnard has bought a

pirogue and this is now being towed alongside the flagship. It will be an interesting exhibit when we return to Britain. The engines have been causing some problems and two crankshafts have broken on Mercurys. Our fitters, Staff-Sergeant Les Winterburn and Corporal Neil Rickard, are working hard to keep them going. The support group, aboard the steamer, have stopped for twenty-four hours at Lisala.

At Kisangani planning continues and I have deployed more people to the otter-shrew party in the forest. Tac HQ dined with Mr and Mrs John Strugnal tonight. We said farewell for tomorrow we fly west to Kinshasa. Roger Chapman's condition continues to fluctuate.

Saturday 14 December

Today Tac HQ moved to Kinshasa by Air Zaire. Lunched with our Defence Attaché. De-briefed FST/A on their recce of Inga rapids. This has gone well although they could not penetrate beyond Inga. Apparently river is very high but beginning to drop. It appears there are some rapids and waterfalls that we shall not be able to navigate, and we must therefore make preparations for several portages. As the river drops, more rapids may appear. I consider that the best conditions for navigation will be in early January. The jet craft have certainly done a magnificent job, and are the first boats ever to have gone downstream from Kinshasa to Inga and back again!

Saw Roger Chapman, who looked absolutely ghastly, and met Dr Bill Close, Pam Baker's former boss, who has been looking after Roger at his own house. Bill is a fascinating and very charming man, and somewhat unusual in that he is an American who went to Harrow. I had heard much of him and his family and consider that the expedition is most fortunate to have met them. Bill told me that Pam has probably saved Roger's life.

A most unfortunate report has appeared in the British

press indicating that there are morale problems on the expedition. Nothing could be further from the truth and of course it has upset many people on the expedition. I spoke strongly to the correspondent about this tonight. It is most important that everyone on the expedition should work towards harmony rather than do anything, however unintentional, that disrupts the community spirit.

Fleet continues to sail westward, apparently beginning to look like an Indian bazaar as the members purchase paddles, pots, canoes, and various items of native art *en route*. Hospitality from everyone along the river grows daily.

Sunday 15 December

Tac HQ occupies a very pleasant apartment in Kinshasa. From here we shall plan the final phase of expedition, that is to take us from the capital to the Atlantic. Spent much time discussing river with jet-boat team, most of whom come from New Zealand. They are experienced people and have done very well on their reconnaissance which is now going to prove extremely useful in the planning of this phase. Long discussions far into night. Only problem seems to be over film copyright which it is difficult to reconcile. Because original company with whom all negotiations were carried out relating to jet boats has now apparently ceased to have interest in matters, am therefore discussing details with parent company in New Zealand and having to start from square one.

Communications with fleet proving difficult. Mike Gambier reports that their battery charger has broken down and they are now having to generate all power by hand. Fifteen minutes on this infernal machine is a real test of muscle!

Support group passed fleet but were unable to resupply as huge container had accidentally been placed on top of hold containing rations and resupply items. This leaves fleet in difficult position as they were expecting four days' rations at this point. Fleet now seven days' sailing from Kinshasa but with little more than one day's supplies. Economy measures have been put in hand and I will try to bring them more rations by Beaver on 17 December. Hospitality at Mbandaka marvellous, local Lions Club and Wimpey Company being extremely kind.

Monday 16 December

Carried out air recce on Inga in Beaver this morning. Water certainly impressive, but is dropping and looking a little easier than when jet boats went through a week ago.

Finances really in desperate state and I was most relieved when I saw Dr Ngwete, the Zaire Minister of Health, who has been assigned to look after the interests of the expedition. He promised to let me have a very generous grant of 5200 zaires towards the cost of looking after his scientists and the LOs who have been with us. The Minister asks that any film of Freddie Rodger's should be shown to him before finally published. He is worried about one or two reports from a local journalist that Freddie is 'acting as a second Stanley'. I don't pretend to understand this rather strange accusation but assured him that we would co-operate to the full. Dr Ngwete is an extremely intelligent, understanding and charming man who has already done a great deal to assist us. We are indeed fortunate to have him as a friend and adviser.

Using radio in GKN office, spoke to Mike Gambier at Mbandaka. Rations still very short. We are doing utmost to relieve this and I plan to fly to the fleet tomorrow. HQ worked late on planning and mail came in at midnight brought by the indefatigable Corporal Winterbottom of the Royal Engineers postal section. This young NCO has worked non-stop and done a wonderful job. With mail came more recriminations on the press report about morale. It appears that next of kin have been upset. At a time when we are trying to raise funds and assure people that their confidence in the expedition is well founded, this report is most unfortunate.

I have finished essence of my outline plan for the final operation to take us to the sea and left a number of reconnaissance tasks to be carried out on the ground in my absence.

Tuesday 17 December

Pam Baker and I flew to join fleet by Beaver this morning. Adrianne Damgaard will return to help nurse Roger Chapman. At Mbandaka we met personnel of Wimpey who have done so much to assist and are very hospitable. They gave us good breakfasts. Apparently fleet stayed with them and had wonderful party last night. The recce section has waited for us and took us downstream; we eventually reached fleet near Gombe and I was able to brief them on the developments and future plans of the expedition. During night rain fell in sheets. Very cold. Strangely there were many mosquitoes. Fleet's morale extremely high but a number of people incensed by press report on their morale being low. Communications continued to be poor, very difficult to get through. Nearby radio station which sounds like Chinese, and may well be, is interfering on our frequency. One or two minor problems to sort out with LOs; nothing serious.

Gombe a rather seedy frontier town, but people friendly. Due to many islands on river, navigation difficult, but Squadron Leader Mike Barnard doing a very good job.

Wednesday 18 December

Awoke this morning with mild fever, feeling very sleepy. Had intended to hold conference of captains on flagship but river was terribly choppy with waves two feet high making progress rather slower than usual. On flagship we were constantly soaked with water and therefore no con-

B

ference possible. Spent day discussing with Mike Gambier. In evening stopped at Morebu-Moke where we met English missionaries, and local people put on fine display of dancing for us. Fever felt better in evening. Today we saw three seagulls, a long way from the sea but a hopeful sign!

Thursday 19 December

Communications again very bad and no contact with base. Cannot understand why this should be. Sergeant John Connor, US Army signaller, did everything he could to get through. Much interference from 'Chinese' station. I suspect this is to our north in neighbouring Congo Republic.

Conference of captains held this morning. Discussed composition of crews for final phase. Little argument and already most skippers had ideas on who they wanted on their boats. We must keep numbers down to minimum as boats required to be very lightly laden.

Airdrop in late afternoon of extra rations which will just get us to Kinshasa. Communication with aircraft not possible, and drop made on outskirts of village where cargo was found by two of our Zaire scientists, Citoyen Kamali (geologist) and Citoyen Kagabo (anthropologist).

Feverish night, sleep difficult, wonder if I have malaria although it doesn't feel much like it.

Friday 20 December

Continued along river, getting wider all the time but still punctuated by long jungle-covered islands. Plenty of floating water-weed and hyacinth. Fish also plentiful. A very monotonous day but thankfully without waves. Myself feeling very grim, fever rising, pains in thighs and chest. Felt better towards the evening and spent night in small bungalow near beach, kindly provided by local people. Communications now obliterated by torrent of Chinese from Congo shore. This frequency of 4500 Mhz is not a good choice.

Saturday 21 December

Moved ahead in recce sections boats with Peter Marett. Feeling very sleepy and rather ill. Found it difficult to write notes. River narrowed again shortly after we started and we were almost mesmerized into landing on Congo Republic bank by mistake. Small villages; jungle now decreasing; river fairly slow; islands of weed drifting downstream. At 1300 hours we reached Kinshasa where we met jet team. Moved to flat, saw Dr Bill Close and Roger Chapman. Bill asked if I felt ill. I replied I was a little hot so he took my temperature which was 104·5°F. Apparently I have a variety of malaria. Quick injection, then off to bed. Adrianne Damgaard and Valerie Jones nursed me. Thankfully, high temperature soon began to drop; still felt pretty rough but my mind became active and I found it difficult to sleep thinking of all the various problems that face us. Report from the Inga Rapids is that they are still high and quite impassable.

Meanwhile fleet is coming on at best speed after us. Mike Gambier reports river now running at 6 km per hour. Weather misty and cold. *Barclays Bank* Mercury engine broke a piston. They are now down to one spare engine. Morale still high although crews a little apprehensive of the waters ahead. Fleet should reach Kinshasa tomorrow. Grand reception planned. Arrangements in Kinshasa are excellent, thanks to Captain Mike Heathcote, Captain Paul Turner and WO 1 Jim Winter. Base parties and signallers have really worked extremely hard to pave the way for us. The Royal Signals team at base, under Sergeant Alan Cobb, have also done a fine job in maintaining our communications to Britain where they are received by the men of 8th Signal Regiment at Catterick.

Sunday 22 December

My temperature down at dawn thanks to Propoquine injection yesterday. Felt weak but all right. Boats arrived in morning and I gave them a short pep talk before they sailed ceremoniously into the Bralima beach for reception at 1400 hrs. The British Ambassador attended and everyone in high spirits. Quite a holiday atmosphere. Local press and TV present. Event extremely well organized by Paul Turner.

Bad news from Beaver, oil leak now limiting flying to maximum of five hours between inspections. We cannot afford to be without this vital part of the expedition at this moment. My main work now is to analyse all reports and plan the details for the assault on the Livingstone Falls. Must avoid too many long portages, as these will be very tiring. Men not really physically fit after long river passage. I foresee at least five of the big falls will be impassable. Mike Gambier says fleet will require at least ten days' work to get boats in good order, but already the jet boat team are talking of returning early to New Zealand; quite why they came all this way knowing that they had to go back early I do not understand. Apparently they have a commercial contract to fulfil in their home country. We certainly need these boats for safety and reconnaissance in the next stretch.

Monday 23 December

Held conference of all group leaders this morning, very useful. Felt ill during conference and temperature rose again, so had second dose of Propoquine; also full blood chemistry test. Better pm.

We are now flat out, preparing boats and carrying out reconnaissance. Engines all need complete overhaul, which will take ten days. Do not think we can afford all this time and must speed things up by some means. Most members are accommodated at the American school, which is extremely comfortable and weatherproof. Others are housed in flats and apartments in and around the Kinshasa. The problem is the transport shortage and simply communicating with everyone.

Valerie Jones taken ill today. She has been moved to hospital and Pam Baker is looking after her. Scientist Sinclair Dunnett also sick, as is Captain Richard Skaife. Dr John Chapman-Smith has now gone home so we have no doctor with us here. However, a local American doctor, Dr Bob Turk, has volunteered to some with us on final phase. At the moment I have Viv Jones at Kisangani, and Freddie Rodger is still in the Kananga region. As he is senior medical officer, it would be useful if I could consult him now. We have tried on many occasions to get through by radio but the distance is too great for our A14. So I am turning more to Dr Bill Close for advice on medical matters in this area.

Tuesday 24 December

Christmas Eve. Valerie Jones better this morning. Boat preparations continue and I was able to visit most outlying units including our radio station at the Calico Printers Association factory, known to all as CPA. Communications to Kisangani are good. Spoke to Nigel Warren regarding medical problems and my concern for the rise in malaria casualties. Dr Bill Close has advised me that we should change from Paludrine to Nivaquine. Local doctors believe this is the answer to the particular brand of malaria found in Zaire. Am unable to get through to Freddie Rodger to confirm that he agrees.

Friends from Britain, the Oatens, arrived in time to join us for the expedition Christmas dinner. This had been laid on at the American School and was quite excellent. Jim Masters and his boys had done most of the cooking and everyone was in good heart. LOs attended. Spent a short time at Bill Close's house visiting Roger Chapman and returned in time for midnight mass, conducted by our chaplain, Basil Pratt. There were forty-one communicants and Basil had to use brandy and Christmas cake as wine and bread were absent. After this we sang carols round fire.

Wednesday 25 December

Christmas Day. The only free day during the whole expedition. Valerie had been transferred back to flat and was a little better, though still quite ill. Lunched in local restaurant before, like most members of expedition, being invited out to local family. We were fed like fighting cocks although, recovering from malaria, I did not feel terribly hungry. Hospitality given to us by local people has again been quite overwhelming.

Thursday 26 December

Went on jet reconnaissance of Kinsuka rapids this morning. Most impressed with fantastic performance of these craft. Jon Hamilton from Hamilton Jets, son of inventor, is a very fine driver, and his American friend, Ralph Brown, is also very good. We got right into the big water where Ralph's boat was swamped and almost came to grief. This water is certainly most impressive and the waves are about six metres high in centre of river. I think we can get through by slipping down on the Zaire side of the rapids. The reconnaissance boats can use a channel behind Mimosa, a convenient island. If they cannot get through there then they must portage.

Friday 27 December

More jet recces continue today. Problem is that transport is in such short supply that it is difficult to move everybody about in the Kinshasa area. Small picnic held on beach with beer kindly provided by Bralima Breweries plus J & B and Merrydown. From this vantage point various group leaders sallied forth in the jet craft to examine rapids. We also made what is believed to be the first ever visit to an island in mid-river called Monkey Island. I can understand why no one could have got there before because it is right in the middle of the rapids, and only a jet could make it by water. Everyone enjoyed their time on these fast highly manoeuvrable boats. Heavy rain fell later in the day accompanied by thunder and lightning.

Saturday 28 December

Boat trials were due to take place today off the Chanimetal dock, where we have received much assistance. Discovered that the second engine, now mounted amidships on the giant craft is not much help for steering but it certainly does give power in the desired direction, once the steering engine at the stern has pointed the craft the right way. We practised using jets to pull and push the giant craft but found it was of limited value. The drill for rescuing people from the water, using a net hung down the side of the jet, was also practised.

Noticed that the rapids have dropped one and a half metres in last two weeks and waves are certainly diminished. Therefore not quite so worried about the immediate water in area of Kinsuka, but new rapids may occur as a result of this drop in level.

Beaver aircraft now completely unserviceable due to the oil leak which has got much worse, and so crew are stripping down to investigate.

The TV boys are having accommodation problems, had to move them out to the school. In some ways it is easier to run the expedition when it is away from the big towns. We are not bogged down with complicated administrative matters.

I foresee a need to have a representative from the expedition in Britain to cope with all our arrangements on return. Undoubtedly there will be more work than Jill Henderson and our small office staff in London can manage. Bill Coleridge is best man to send on in advance as he works in London and has contacts there.

I can well imagine Stanley's feelings when he faced the first of the cataracts after coming all the way from Kisangani in his fleet of craft. The rapids look bad enough to me so goodness knows what they looked like to him in his frail wooden boats. Constantly attacked by hostile tribes, bothered by heat and insects, anxious about the cataracts that lay ahead, and carefully conserving his last remaining goods and weapons, Stanley moved slowly down the broad, slow-flowing river.

February 21st: On the morning of the 19th, we regarded each other mostly as destined victims of protracted famine, or the rage of savage natives. But as we feared famine most, we determined to try the natives. We saw a few fishermen on an island and mildly showed our several kinds of monies to them. Cloth, beads, wire, copper, ivory, iron, et cetera. They frightened ran to the woods, bawling out some words which we could not understand. Two miles further came to a small island opposite a settlement, and without paying regard to the small canoes plying about, we beached our canoes and began to build a camp. Presently a canoe with 7 men came dashing across and we prepared with monies in view of them, unhesitatingly beached their canoes amongst our own [*sic*]. This was one sure auspicious sign of confidence. We were liberal, the natives fearlessly accepted beads and shells we gave them, and then went a step further; we sealed this growing peace with the ceremony of blood brotherhood and interchange of gifts. Still the first day food came but slowly, as there were three Chiefs to be satisfied... the second day food came abundantly and on the 21st goats, wine were added to our necessities. Cloth was the universal demand. Black, Red, and Blue blanketry, Madrassees, Merikani, Kaniki, handkerchiefs and Kitambis. Brass tacks, brass bands, wire, plates, cups, knives, looking glasses. All had guns, old American flintlocks, overloaded with brass bands and brass tacks, and, worn suspended by broad bands of the red buffalo hide, murderously long knives.

It was most difficult to understand them, but we did very well with signs. It was also difficult task to induce one native to stay long enough for a social chat. But on the morning of the third day, trade lagging, one was discovered patient enough to sit and give such information as I desired.

My notebook was in great demand and would have found a ready sale, they called it Tara Tara or Looking-glass, which they believed came from above.

Stanley resumed his voyage and it is interesting to see that soon after he noted in the corner of a sketch-map for the day's journey:

February 24th: Hippopotamus attacked a canoe and snatched a paddle from a man's hand, and almost upset the heaviest canoe we had. I believe he was so ferocious at sight of the donkeys, believing they were young of his tribe.

March 8th: Our journey today has been about 12 miles.

We started with the guides from Chumbiri with fair hopes that we should continue together, that they should be faithful to their trust. They had performed ceremonies during the night to appease their God and to induce him to give them his protection on the journey. About 8 am a violent rainstorm lasting 4 hours began. Noon we tried it again, but an hour afterwards they halted again and told us to continue on. Though suspecting strongly that they were intending to leave us, we proceeded until nearly sunset. In the night a boa constrictor 12 feet long was seen advancing towards one of the men. The man hailed it thinking it to be a man as it raised itself, and asked who it was, but instantly perceived his mistake and screamed: 'A serpent! A serpent!' At the noise the boa glided away, but in about half an hour was seen in another part of the camp, and this time after a good deal of noise was despatched.

On the 9 March 1877 Stanley's expedition fought their thirty-second battle. During the fight four of his own men were wounded, but they drove off their attackers and proceeded on their way. On 13 March he found that the river was suddenly widening into a great pool. Learning that there were cataracts ahead he camped and commenced his reconnaissance.

March 13th: Halt above Cataract.

At about noon the river widened until it resembled a Lake with numerous sandy bars, islets, and several wooded islands. On the right bank there was a wall of cliffs – chalk – resembling Dover Cliffs so greatly that I have named them after them in order to distinguish and guide the future traveller.

Then descending along the right bank near the first Falls opposite Ntamo we encountered very peaceable people in canoes who spoke kindly and came near, unsuspicious and confident, to us, to speak with us which we took to be a good omen. A little above the first breaking of the water we camped . . .

Stanley had now followed the river for 1235 miles from where he had first joined it at Nyangwe. The pool where he now camped was in future to be known as Stanley Pool, and he named the falls below this pool after Dr David Livingstone. Today Kinshasa, capital of Zaire, overlooks the Stanley Pool from the south and Brazzaville, capital of the Congo Republic, overlooks the same pool from the north shore. At 4 pm on 15 March 1877 Stanley began his descent of the Livingstone Falls. On Sunday 29 December 1974 the Zaire River Expedition was still continuing its preparations.

First cataract, Livingstone Falls

Sunday 29 December

Roger Chapman very poorly this morning. Saw him briefly; he really is having a rough time and is being very brave about it. A busy day on visits. The personnel at Kisangani are complaining about being sent the wrong anti-malaria drugs.

There is much activity throughout the expedition in preparing for what I call Operation Rubicon. This is to be the final advance, which I hope will take us to the Atlantic. Held a co-ordinating conference at 1700 hours and the members seemed very keen to be off. Tac HQ is full of people licking and sticking stamps on to our special covers which we hope to sell after the expedition. Money is very tight and our fund-raising goes on non-stop.

Monday 30 December

Sick rate is rising rapidly; more are now down with dysentery and malaria. Am finding it difficult to fill all the appointments that we need to run Operation Rubicon. Boat trials going well and the power with the two engines is now excellent. *David Gestetner* is behaving like a speed boat! Ken Monk of Gestetner, who did so much to help get this expedition launched, would be very proud of her.

There was no air recce today because of the problems with the Beaver. Two engines were unserviceable and the administration is lagging behind so I decided to postpone the start of Operation Rubicon for twenty-four hours. One of the problems of communication with Kisangani is that messages seem to continuously cross over; we must try to sort this out. Have now asked Viv Jones to move up here as medical officer. There is much sickness in Kisangani but Freddie Rodger should be able to cope. Among the sick are Ernie Durey's engineer section. This is a blow as I foresee the need for them in the next stretch.

More problems about the morale report in the British

press. Many letters from home complain about it. Am eager to get away from Kinshasa where I feel we may be out-staying our welcome. We tend to descend like a plague of locusts wherever we go, scrounging everything we can to make up for our lack of equipment, transport and funds. Captain Alun Davies RRW, who has been commanding the recce section, is very concerned that he has now to use Johnson outboard engines because the Mercurys are all required for the giant craft, but after running with the Johnsons for a couple of days his fears have been put aside. They have the advantage of being lighter but are not so waterproof as the Mercurys.

Tuesday 31 December

Have been suffering bad attack of dysentery for several days but better now. Final preparations for Rubicon in hand. I am still worried about the communications; it is always a problem on this expedition. Sick rate still rising, Corporal Hamer now has what is thought to be flu. Frustrations of being in Kinshasa are beginning to tell and one or two mild personality clashes have occurred, including one today between FST/C and the boat crews. I noticed that few subordinates are ready to air their grievances to me but instead grumble amongst themselves. This must be cor-rected if unity is to be maintained.

  Peter Marett is doing a wonderful job preparing all the advanced intelligence of the stretch that lies ahead. We have been studying every known report, including some of Stan-ley's, in order to glean information on the location and severity of the rapids. As the water continues to drop, more rapids are certainly appearing, but the general consensus of opinion is that the water is getting easier and I now think it may be possible to get through all but four stretches. The trouble is that one of the rapids which we may have to portage is in a chasm, and the portage will be extremely difficult. But if we can run through this one, known as

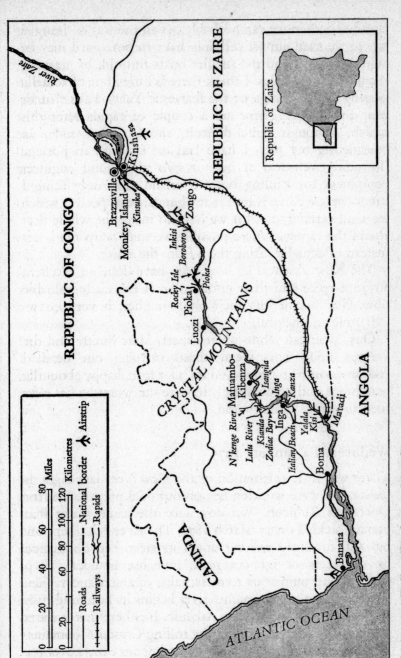

Livingstone Falls – Kinshasa to Matadi

Boroboro, then we can probably get all the way to Isangila where we shall almost certainly have to portage. I may be able to get jets and the smaller boats through by warping them down the sides. I think there is little hope of actually passing through Inga or the fearsome Yalala Falls that lie near to Matadi. There are a couple of rapids after this which, although quite difficult, should be possible. In considering my plan I have laid on facilities to portage (including vehicles) at one or two places and engineer equipment for hauling boats overland. The only thing I cannot arrange in advance is an abundance of porters which we shall certainly need if we have to move the whole fleet round the rapids. Where possible we shall warp the boats instead of actually lifting them from the water.

The New Zealand jet boat team have done an excellent advance recce and their information is especially valuable now. Guy Mannering, their photographer, is very knowledgeable and helpful.

Our American white water expert, Marc Smith, and the various FSTs have been ahead carrying out detailed reconnaissance on ground, Marc is far from happy about the conditions and he confesses they are the worst he has ever seen anywhere in the world.

Wednesday 1 January 1975

There was little celebration of the New Year last night as most of us were working late on our final preparations for Operation Rubicon. We now face the same water that Stanley tackled on 15 March 1877. The river is higher now but still furiously rushing down its steep bed obstructed by the reefs of igneous rock, immense boulders, deep canyons and numerous terraces, falls, cataracts and rapids. For it is here that the mighty river begins its headlong rush from the Zaire basin to the Atlantic. It is here that it starts to carve its passage through the rolling Crystal Mountains.

Today I felt the real culmination of all our efforts over the last four years. Now we shall discover if our reconnaissance has been correct, our designs adequate and our preparations efficient. For everything we have done before is now belittled by this terrifying stretch of water that like a mighty ocean, thunders away in a mass of waves and foam on its course to the sea. Stanley was forced to portage round almost all the major obstacles in this next stretch, but I believe that by using our various types of craft we should be able to pass at least half the rapids. Already the advanced reconnaissance team using the jet boats have managed to get as far as Inga and return safely, and I should accordingly be able to use the giant inflatables for much of the way. I am, however, concerned with one or two of the rapids beyond MK (Mafuambo-Kibenza) Ferry and it may be prudent to remove the giant craft there and continue the advance by jet and recce boat. Derek Jackson has geared his support to this possibility.

Final preparations completed by 1100 hours. Jets despatched into first rapid to stand by as safety boats. Skippers had last look at water and the advance commenced. Sent Close recce section by a side channel to miss the worst of the water. Giants ordered forward; *La Vision, Barclays Bank,* and *David Gestetner* last. *La Vision* passed through safely. The camera and press team situated on isolated rock in excellent position. Large crowd on shore, and President

Mobutu understood to be watching from the lawns of the Presidential Palace!

At approximately 1200 hours *David Gestetner* entered rapid. As she crossed first five-foot ledge, her stern motor was flipped up, possibly by a rock; transom broke and engine came adrift with its thrashing propeller slicing through the neoprene of the stern compartment. Rapid deflation followed. The engine on its safety line fell into the water and the boat lost steerage immediately. The stricken craft was then carried into the coffee-coloured foaming waves that hurled about in the centre of the passage. Midships engine still running and I observed Lieutenant John Watkin trying to steer with it. To little avail. Ordered Jet 1, in which I was travelling, to go to the rescue. At same time noted *Barclays Bank* had stopped and was shadowing us.

Marc Smith had realized danger and was standing by. National Panasonic VHF radios were invaluable and enabled the emergency plans to be put into action immediately. Jon Hamilton, skipper of Jet 1, took our craft into the towering waves with great skill and courage. For a few seconds it seemed that we too would be overcome. Then suddenly, from behind an enormous roller, the stricken *Gestetner* appeared almost on top of us. Giant waves lifted the great silver craft high in the air and it crashed down upon us. Fortunately, being soft, no damage. Jet 1 wriggled from beneath the giant inflatable and we circled once again. Saw Mike Gambier in water trying to swim towards Jet 2 which had emergency scramble-net down the side. Gambier rescued; apparently he had left *Gestetner* on skipper's orders to lighten ship, extremely brave! On second pass, managed to take line from Corporal Qarau and then jet towed crippled craft through the raging cataracts and beached it on Monkey Island. Damage inspected and found to be repairable. Giant inflatable then towed to south bank of river near CPA factory for repairs. I was very pleased with the conduct of all personnel and the expertise with which the emergency plans were carried out. Without the power of the jets, there might have been serious loss of life. Crews frightened but elated, press and television ecstatic!

Twenty-four hours should be given for repairs. Intend to wait until late tomorrow morning. Beaver flew air recce forward this afternoon and reported no significant change ahead. A few administrative problems of resupply, mainly caused by our lack of transport.

Thursday 2 January

During planning stages of this expedition I noted that in common with most great rivers it appeared navigation would be easier at high water. Stanley himself had extremely difficult passage on the few rapids he could manage, because he struck this area when water level was low; i.e., in March/April.

The CPA staff were extremely helpful and repaired transom for the *David Gestetner* in their workshops. Started late after repairs completed, waving farewell to our CPA friends, and headed downriver in swirling currents. Jet 1 had returned to Kinshasa for fuel and I therefore advanced in Jet 2. Engine trouble, due to a fish net entangled in the impellor shortly after start, caused one hour's delay and was only cleared after determined efforts by Ralph Brown.

Shot rapids at tail end of Kinsuka. Stanley wrote of these as the 'Mother', 'Father' and 'Child' rapids. We also cleared the Lady Alice and Foulakari rapids. No great problems but river almost like a living animal, boiling, bubbling, swirling and hissing about us. The coffee-coloured water rushes on towards the sea. Must be a high degree of organic material in the water that gives it this colour.

Have deliberately lightened boats to absolute minimum, and therefore carry little food or fuel. Our engines are essential if we are to pick our way through the cataracts, so fuel drops and resupply points have been arranged. Beaver

Below the Lady Alice rapids

landed fuel at Zongo airstrip tonight. This was collected by FST/C and brought to the river. Unfortunately, Beaver did not go on ahead to do air reconnaissance. This was a confounded nuisance and left me in an ill temper.

Camped just above Inkisi rapid, on idyllic beach near picturesque waterfall. At Inkisi river junction passed large islands alive with huge bats. Literally thousands of them took off when I deliberately fired a flare into the trees which were festooned with these hideous creatures. They flew about for many minutes showering down their excreta. Stanley reported great flocks of birds in this area, but I wonder if what he saw were in fact these huge bats. They have a twelve-inch wing span and rat-like bodies. They returned to nest in trees after being disturbed. Noted very large bat traps and nets on both banks of the river. Understand natives catch and eat them. Total distance run today:

65 km; ended with camp at Teba river junction, at 1545 hours.

La Vision transom split and repaired. Seems to be a weakness in our design. Johnson 40 hp motors tend to oil up, may be plug trouble.

River banks now steep and gorges frequent. Water very turbulent and current rapid. In many places backwash in river goes as far upstream as it does down. Night location: 04°44·2'S, 14°52·2'E. Crews are now much happier with their craft as the inflatables glide with the current over even the biggest waves. Giants very stable. Extra engine ideal. We are able to move across the river in a way I had at one time thought impossible. There is still the problem of stopping in fast water but we seem to be managing rather better than I had thought we would.

By 23 April 1877 Stanley estimated he had covered thirty-five miles of rapids, falls and cataracts. It had taken him thirty-seven days; the Zaire River Expedition had made the journey in two days. The trials and tribulations suffered by Stanley's team are illustrated in his diary.

Portaging the first cataract of the Livingstone Falls

March 16th: Continued on our work and descended half a mile or ¾ of a mile to the River Juemba which issues into the Congo from the right bank just at the Falls. We have some skilful work to do to dare the mighty current round the rocky points, and lower the canoes by hawsers, which, had one broken, would have certainly been the destruction of the canoe and the men in it, for only a few yards below rushes the river with enormous leaping waves into a brown abyss of mad waters and rocks and foam. Having arrived in the Juemba we paddled desperately across to an island and here our labours ended for the day.

March 17th: Dragged the canoes across Juemba Island to the western branch of the Juemba River, distance about 800 yards. Chief of Bateke Manoweh visited me and for a small gratuity of cloth repaid with a small supply of food' became fast friends. People very hungry. If none can be procured tomorrow we must despatch the riding asses.

March 18th: Descended the west branch of the Juemba River to its junction with the Congo about half a mile and then camped. People faint for lack of food. We had to stay work to allow them to hunt for food. They were successful and made tolerably good marketing. A goat is not to be seen in the country and a chicken is to be esteemed the value of a gun, but cassava is abundant.

March 19th: Crossed the point of land with the canoes which is west of the confluence of the Juemba and Congo, and placed the canoes in a creek. The natives continue friendly although the numerous chiefs are expensive. However they bring us food and so long as matters stand thus, we may be content. Accidents were numerous the first day. One dislocated his shoulder, another cut his foot badly on the rough rocks, legs and feet were cut.

Struggling and heaving with his boats, Stanley moved on downriver. After a short rest he started work again.

March 25th: We set to work at daybreak with the canoes to lower them down the Rapids, but alas we were only able to do half a mile. We lost our best canoe, 75 feet long and 3 feet wide by 21 inches deep, the Rapids were too strong for us. At evening a canoe parted from us was upset, sent back half a mile, sent to the current, again ejected half a mile and finally to our great joy secured. Another canoe was almost totally ruined but we have patched it up and it may serve. Horrible and slow work. All my energies are engaged in it.

March 26th: Got 5 canoes and boat down Cauldron to Camp near Rocky Island. Our best remaining canoe broke its cane cables as we lowered it, was swept down the Cauldron, heaved up, whirled round in quick gyrations and finally sent into bay near our camp where it was finally secured. One Chief had his great toe crushed, a man was pitched on his head by the waves, and while turning round after the fearful day's labour I suddenly dropped down to my astonishment into a pit among the great rocks 25 feet deep, escaping thankfully with my life, with only a few rib bruises to remind me that it was bad policy to be careless in such dangerous places.

March 28th: Lowered canoes down to bend opposite Rocky Island and Falls.

The great river of Congo which we but late admired for its lake-like breadth on which we glided so smoothly is now a maddened flood, its free flow restrained by huge walls of basaltic bolders and caked lava. It roars its anger incessantly, and bounds down its steep interrupted bed like a contracted angry sea between cliffs.

March 29th: From this bend at daybreak we began to punt the canoes close to the rocks until we reached the Falls, then cut bushes and overlaid a point of rocks with them and made a kind of tramway, for in this work we were now experienced. By noon we had crossed the point with our 13 canoes and boat all of which were got safely and without accident in a little cove protected by the Rocky Point. Our next labour was apparently easy. I had sent a man the day previous to examine the river as far as the bend where we intended to camp, and he reported that by clinging to the right bank there was not the slightest danger. I instructed the people to keep close to the right bank and by no means to venture into the strong heaving current. This, 'Please God', they proposed to do.

The boat as usual led the way and got safely into the bend, followed by 3 canoes. The fourth canoe over 80 feet long was manned by six paddlers [one of these was a boy named Kalulu who had long served with Stanley] . . . Rehani the steersman did not observe my instructions, the current wafted him slowly into the middle of the mighty river where human strength availed nothing and the canoe and its unfortunate people glided by over the treacherous calm surface like an arrow to doom. It soon reached the island which cleft the Falls, and swept to the left branch, was whirled round three or four times, and presently we saw the stern of the canoe pointed upward and knew then that only by a miracle could any of the crew be saved.

Fast upon this catastrophe, before we could begin to wail their loss, another canoe with two men darted by, borne by like lightning on the bosom of the placid but irresistible waters to apparent nay almost certain destruction. We shouted out to them commands to make for the left shore. 'Inshallah,' the steersman replied, and vigorously the two men set to work. By a strange chance or his dexterity, he shot his canoe over the Falls, and lowered down in calmer water he contrived to secure his canoe to the shore.

The two men were presently seen clambering over the rocks towards the point opposite our camp, and finally to sit down regarding us in silence, so far as we knew. Our pity and love gushed strong towards them, but we could utter nothing of it. The roar of the Falls mocked and overpowered the feeble human voice.

In the hope to save the rest of the canoes, for there were still two behind, 8 having arrived safely, I despatched a messenger to instruct the crews not to trust to their paddles alone but to have in each small canoe two men to tow the canoe by cane ropes on shore and two in each canoe with paddles and poles to keep from striking against rocks. The messenger returned with their reply that they would observe all precaution, but he had no sooner done speaking than a third canoe darted past with only one man, a young fellow called Soudi of Ituru who knew nothing of steering, but who paddled his canoe as if by instinct. As he passed us, he shouted to me: 'I am lost, Master; there is but one God'. He then was seen to address himself to what Fate had in store for him.

The river swept him down, down over the First Falls, then gave him a breathing pause in dead water, again caught him and his canoe in its tremendous force, precipitated him down, over the second and the third and fourth falls, great waves meanwhile striking madly at him, and yet his canoe did not sink, but he and it were seen to sweep behind the island and we could see nothing more, for darkness fell on us and on the river.

It is said that the cause of this last accident was the faithlessness of the crew. One man, unnerved by what he saw, ran away and hid in the bushes, another let go the tow rope, and the other rope, too weak to resist the sudden forces and weight, snapped, and thus the man is probably lost.

During the night a large canoe was swept from its mooring by a sudden tide, and this has closed our losses for this day.

We have now but 9 canoes and the boat left, inadequate to carry the Expedition. Some of the people must, therefore, go on land.

Stanley's hazardous but slow progress down this terrifying waterway continued. How he survived himself is quite amazing for he had many narrow escapes.

April 12th: The others let go, fearing the same fate, the bow cable parted and the boat with me, two boys and two men, was flying down the mighty and terrible stream borne on the crest of great waves, whirled round like a spinning top, diving into threatening troughs, and swirling pits, then jostled aside, uplifted by another wave and tossed upon the summit of another, while the shore was flying by us with amazing rapidity, which we could not reach. The boat also leaked so badly to which we could give no attention that was another element of danger.

We soon came in view of a bend in the land where I had purposed to camp, and below the river looked wilder than ever. Could we but get within the influence of the eddy tide, we might be saved. We devoted all our energies to enter within its influence, across the swift gliding waters.

As we began to feel that it was useless to contend with the current, a sudden terrible rumbling noise caused us to look below, and we saw the river almost heaved bodily upward, as if a volcano had burst under it. It took the form of a low shapeless mound, and presently half of the mass approached us in lines of white breakers, gurgling bodies separated by so many whirling pools, one of which caught and embraced our poor shattered way-worn boat, by which we were spun around and around and around with the stern threatening each moment to drop into the

The Lady Alice *over the falls*

centre of the wide pit, until finally we were spun out of it into the
ebb tide and so were saved. The people were almost in despair
and were rushing after us distractedly, but long before they
reached us they met a man whom I sent to inform them of our
safety.

The man who was dragged into the water, I saved.

On 19 April 1877 Stanley thought he had arrived at
Yalala, but still there was news of more cataracts ahead.
His maps were undoubtedly very inaccurate. This was his
major problem for he had to rely entirely on local people for
information, and many of the tribesmen only knew their
immediate areas. Food was always a great worry for him,
and as his trading goods diminished he came nearer to
starvation. The river that the 1974 expedition faced was
every bit as dangerous, but our equipment was a great
improvement on Stanley's and we also had the benefit of
extremely reliable reconnaissance and good maps.

Friday 3 January

Distance covered: 21 km. Camp site: 04°52·5'S, 14°42·5'E. Nearest town: Mvuanza. The scenery is magnificent with cliffs on sides of the gorges up to eighty metres in height. There were bands of black basalt in the sandstone at the sides of the river. Snakes were seen swimming, and one small orange-red viper with pointed scales and a pale yellow underside was caught by Richard Snailham.

Major rapids navigated were Inkisi and then the dreaded Boroboro. Later we navigated an unnamed rapid which was not too severe. The river continues to drop and has fallen approximately thirty centimetres in twenty-four hours. Boroboro was most formidable rapid we have tackled yet. I did not dare to take the Avon S400s through, manned, and ordered them to be towed by jets into centre of current and released unmanned. This did not work too well as there is such a strong current going upstream that they were continuously carried back, but, after some skilful manoeuvring we got them through. Went through in Jet 1 with my HQ, waves enormous, about nine metres high. Just as we left rapid a great boiling mass of water reared up with a deep rumbling sound right beside us; the mass of water was some two metres in height. As it subsided, the water began to spin wildly. As it accelerated a vortex appeared in the centre and soon we were gazing down a horrific whirlpool some thirty metres across and three metres deep in the centre. The river around us had gone mad, waves breaking, rocks flashing by and all the 220 hp of the jet's engine were called upon to drag us from the grip of this revolving cavern. As we left it the hole closed up again and the surface became a sheet of fast-moving water. Similarly, another giant whirlpool appeared on our right and another ahead. The river was wild and it was almost as if some unseen force was trying to pluck us downwards.

The fleet passed safely through and we camped behind an island which is named Rocky Isle on the map. The beach was scenic and we spent the night on the warm golden sand

Fall of the Edwin Arnold river

beneath a great cliff. Looking eastward from our camp we could see into a wide basin with waterfalls cascading from the high cliffs on either side. I believe that this is where Frank Pocock's body drifted after he was drowned in Boro-boro. Stanley's *Through The Dark Continent* has a drawing of a tall waterfall which he calls the Fall of the Edwin Arnold River. He writes of the basin which we can now see as the Pocock Basin. Near the foot of the fall, there is a large long cave running along the edge of the cliffs. I had originally intended camping inside this but, because of the drop in river, the mooring and anchorage is too poor to risk. Hence my move on to the beach at Rocky Isle. Although the falling water lessens the strength of the river, new problems are being ecnountered daily.

Captain Kabe, our Zaire Navy LO, tells me he was born

near here and local boat-builders who came to visit us knew his village which is some twenty kilometres away.

Saturday 4 January

As is customary, the chiefs of the nearest village called on me shortly after dawn. They were extremely friendly and very glad to see Captain Kabe. They told us that the expedition's boats were the first they had seen on this part of the river and in our honour they would rename this beach, the 'Beach of the Great Boats'. I was presented with a bouquet of wild flowers as a symbol of the New Year and their peaceful intent towards us.

Moved on to Pioka Rapids, a large and possibly dangerous stretch of water. Due to our acute shortage of fuel, we were forced to stop above the cataracts. We then siphoned all the fuel from one jet and put it in the other, which we then sent ahead to make contact with Tom Mabe and his FST who were positioned at the cataract. I sent with them Mike Heathcote and also Lieutenant Nigel Armitage-Smith of the Queen's. Meanwhile we switched on the radio and attempted to make contact with Derek Jackson and the support group that must now be at Luozi. At midday the Beaver appeared and dropped a message to us from Derek confirming his location at Luozi and the presence of fuel there. But, with no large stocks of fuel immediately forward of Pioka, the jet only just managed to reach Luozi, having siphoned all Tom Mabe's Toyota truck's fuel to do it! Jet returned early pm with fuel and fleet negotiated the cataract in grand style. Recce boats put up an especially good performance, using their superior power-weight ratio to side-slip through some of the largest waves we have seen. On land Mike Heathcote apparently missed his pick-up and got lost! I waited forty minutes for him and then had to chase after the giant boats in the jets to avoid a nonsense at the night stop. At Luozi, camped and met support group. All refuelled and heard problems now that two of the FST vehicles have broken down. As usual we are outstripping our support, and it is only by the valiant efforts of Derek Jackson, Dick Festorazzi and our support team that fuel and rations are getting through. Roads reported as being terrible. A major problem is that the jet craft are simply drinking petrol. With all the running up and down river they are doing on reconnaissance, and as safety boats as well, they are dropping down to one and a quarter kilometres to the gallon! So far they have used three times as much fuel as was forecast. Nevertheless their fantastic power is a great asset. No other craft can go upstream against these rapids.

Dr Bob Turk is already treating our sick. Certain amount of ear trouble and minor fever. The report on the way ahead is that there are no problems as far as MK Ferry, but after that the rapids and falls at Isangila are said to be almost impassable. I feel that we must force some of our boats through, and if necessary will go ahead with the recce craft and the jets only. At this stage I cannot risk destroying the giants. This will mean a long, arduous march overland for the crews. It will be especially hard as our feet are soft from immersion in water and muscles are not tuned to long walks in hills.

The camp site tonight was our worst yet. Damp, dirty, smelly, and filled with local people who use this area for washing and toilet facilities. Some big iron wheels have been found nearby. Said to have been used by Stanley for portaging boats!

Sunday 5 January

Reached MK Ferry. The river from Pioka was easy with only a few small rapids, thanks to high water. We passed one or two wrecked barges which we are told were swept downstream from Kinshasa at time of high flood! We were also asked to look out for the body of a man lost when his canoe turned over in Boroboro yesterday. Sending the jets ahead to Isangila we took the giants on the long, rather boring journey down to MK Ferry.

Rendezvoused with jets at MK Ferry and discussed problem of Isangila. Advice from Jim Masters and Marc Smith was that it would be suicidal to attempt Isangila in giant craft. Therefore decided to launch Operation Tusker which would involve proceeding with only jet craft and the two Avon S400s, sending big boats by vehicle to next part that they can cope with. Both crews will have to march! Great care will be necessary with the S400s if they are to be lined and driven through the terrible water ahead.

FST/C brought in two drums of fuel. Messages coming from Kisangani talk of sickness with that portion of the expedition. It is over seventeen hundred kilometres away by river. Communication is not good with them and a number of misunderstandings have arisen because of this. Nigel Warren doing magnificent job there in co-ordinating all scientists and medical teams in the region. The rest of the scientists are either working along the river parallel to us or in Kinshasa. In the forefront of the battle is Dr Alan Bartram who has been with us since the source. He is still collecting his fish fossils and now looking for blind fish in caves. He is a most determined scientist and works tirelessly to achieve his aim. The medical research teams are now completing their task and should be joining us in Kinshasa at the end of the expedition.

We have seen evidence of training camps for Angolan rebels – Chinese instructors. Must be careful to avoid unnecessary contact with these forces in this remote area.

Monday 6 January

Reorganization at MK. The logistic group went back to Kinshasa to collect more stores. More misunderstandings due to poor communication with Kisangani, and now hear that all doctors feel they must come forward! What they wish to do, I am not sure, but as money is so short committee has ordered me not to spend anything unnecessarily and air fares are expensive. More problems from the rear. Letters come from Kinshasa complaining that some accommodation lent to members of the expedition was left in bad order. I wonder if the owners realize the battle we are fighting at this front end; but we are at fault and I have been writing letters of apology today.

Another problem is that the jet-boat team feel they must leave us because of this important contract they have in New Zealand. Fortunately, we are a week ahead of time, and anyway I am not certain if there is a task for them after we reach Inga. I do not relish the thought of portaging jet craft.

Mike Heathcote has been found. Despatched Jim Masters and recce team on Operation Tusker. In afternoon found interesting limestone caves on west bank of river near MK Ferry, apparently caused by erosion. Some bats but no sign of habitation. Took jet boats right inside cave; fascinating. A day of many many problems – political, logistic and personal – but we press on. The river is still the greatest problem of all. Bitten by a scorpion lurking in my rucksack – confounded nuisance!

Tuesday 7 January

Leaving giant craft to be moved by support group we shuttled crews and light scales of equipment forward from MK Ferry to Isangila. Banks of the river consist of stratified rock buckled by enormous pressure. Fascinating sight and I regret that none of our geologists was with me. One crocodile seen but otherwise trip was uneventful.

Even before the great rapid came in sight we could hear

the thunder of its water. Looking ahead we saw a line of foam being tossed skywards amongst the black rock. The Avon recce boats had already passed through by being warped down the side. Apparently there had been an incident when one boat was damaged and Jim Masters injured. But when I reached the cataract we had no idea of the extent of the damage. Jon Hamilton took Jet 1 cautiously up to the edge of the leaping waves. Some of the troughs between them were a hundred metres long, and the foaming brown water plunged forward from one trough to another. At the edge of the first fall the river rushed down into a great trough before gathering itself up into an enormous wave, and then the water rushed on downwards into another trough. The wave towers went on into the distance, each one trying to outdo the other, flinging their foam and spray high into the air, bounding mountains of surf. The noise of the river and the heavy engine made it impossible to communicate except by shouting.

To the left a narrow tongue of smooth water swept by the dark brown cliffs and appeared to give a passage. Depositing TV team and Jon Hamilton's wife Joyce on bank, Jon and Ralph Brown edged their craft into this tongue. I had my cine-camera raised in one hand and with the other hung on to the safety bar for dear life. At first we had a smooth passage and then suddenly through the viewfinder I saw we were rushing down into the bottom of an enormous trough. On either side of us, coming like express trains, were two huge waves. They met with a crash like an explosion on our hull, hurling us high into the air. The blow transmitted itself through my arm and gave a wicked wrench at the shoulder joint. Inside the boat we were thrown about and I ended up crashing down on top of Jon. Momentarily he lost the steering wheel but in a split second had it again. As we crashed back on to the surface of this raging sea I saw to my horror another giant wave, God knows what height it was, tumbling head on towards us. The worst possible conditions for a boat to meet in a rapid.

The next moment we were drenched and shaken by the raging water. How the hull of the craft withstood the impact of the blow I do not know. Pam Baker, who was clutching on behind me, was almost flung over the side. To our horror the engine now began to falter. Water must have reached the plugs. We all knew what would happen if the engine failed now, for ahead of us there lay a line of dragon's teeth rocks through which the cataract was being strained. As the engine stopped Jon Hamilton's hand flew to the starter button. Three times the engine failed, and then it spluttered weakly into life. The power was just enough to get us out of the worst of the current and into the lee of a rocky island in the centre of the river. There we joined Jet 2 who, having got safely through, had watched impotently our terrifying course towards the dragon's teeth. Now the problem was to retrieve the TV crew and Joyce Hamilton from the far side of the rapids.

Following the lightening of Jet 2, Jon Hamilton changed over to it from his own sick craft. Most of us were landed on shore to join up with Jim Masters and his group. Meanwhile escorted by the underpowered craft Jon courageously took the remaining jet back through the water that had nearly destroyed us. Strangely, as he approached the towering waves a fresh flood passed through the gap calming the rough water and turning the passage once more into a smooth tongue. The river, as ever, was completely inconsistent and Jon had no difficulty in retrieving the stranded party.

Back on the beach we noted that the water was surging in and out at almost two-minute intervals. Sometimes the surges were as much as one and a half metres in vertical height. The river was quite literally alive. It will be difficult to explain these conditions to people in Britian who simply cannot comprehend the sheer power of this monster river.

It was growing dark when Jon and the jets pressed on towards Inga. We later heard that he had almost come to grief in another rapid lower down and finally reached safety with only a few drops of fuel left. Thus departed our jets, and the team will return to New Zealand.

One recce boat had a two-metre rip in its bottom, which has been repaired with nine hundred stitches and almost all the spare adhesive that we have. Jim Masters and Sergeant Bob Russell decided to shoot the final rapid in Isangila, but unfortunately they struck a fish trap and Jim was washed out of the craft and then dragged behind it. Apart from a badly bruised back he has recovered. Meanwhile, under Mike Gambier, Boat Party A moved on downstream to recce the next rapid at Kianda, leaving Jim (Boat Party B) and my own Tac HQ to come on with the recce group. During the night a hippo was heard calling near our beach and we have seen one small crocodile in the day. We noted cattle in a fenced field near the river, but none of the natives had any knowledge of the *Lady Alice* which Stanley is said to have dragged up on to a mound and abandoned at this point almost one hundred years ago. Isangila had stopped him, but by a miracle we had got through.

Captain Kabe had already engaged some thirteen porters from the village for three days' work. They came down to see us, bringing a supply of sugar-cane wine in large demijohns. It had a strange bouquet and tasted rather like a sweet sauterne, I preferred the J & B whisky that we had brought with us. An exciting and frightening day that we shall long remember.

Unable to shoot any of the difficult rapids, Stanley's advance through what was to become known as the cataract region was much slower than ours and presented him with many more problems and difficulties.

April 25th: Descend half a mile, then camp. I explore ahead, and perceive no road by river or near its banks. I therefore determine upon a mountain route 1,200 feet high, and point out the path.

April 26th: Hauled 6 canoes up the mountain between sunrise and sunset to the utter amazement of the natives on the tableland who believed that I intended to march the Expedition with a canoe

F

train for the future overland. Our hostile, and fearful friends opposite took position early in the morning to see us shoot the Falls and perish in the brown billows of the Congo, but they have not been able to make up their minds yet why we allowed such a bright day for such a spectacle to pass idly away The six men whom I sent 4 days ago to explore the terrible Cataract reported lately to us, returned today at sunset and were told by fearful natives that the White Chief was carrying his canoes over the mountains, and they were seen locking and tying their hogs up and removing valuable things away further inland, and fastening their doors and preparing with resignation and fortitude for the dreadful results of such a wild undertaking.

The report of my explorers is rather encouraging, but it will not do to build too high hopes upon them, for the principal of them is liable to exaggerate favourably as others of his class are to exaggerate opposite.

In the following days Stanley continued his struggle, pausing to make new canoes out of huge trees.

Having re-equipped his expedition with boats Stanley moved on again. However soon more craft were damaged and more repairs were necessary. The men were also suffering. Frank Pocock was lame from ulcers in his feet. To add to his difficulties Stanley found that his men were constantly feeling even the smallest insect bite. On 1 June 1877 he reached Mowa Cove. And it was near here that tragedy struck once again.

June 3rd: A BLACK WOEFUL DAY! We had all enjoyed a pleasant rest from hard labours and today we were prepared to toil our way through the few remaining Falls without pause until we should reach the calm river a few miles below, and last night Frank Pocock had been called to my tent where we chatted pleasantly and sociably about the near end of our struggles through the Congo Falls, also of the hopeful termination of our many dangerous toils. Frank had been for many days a victim to ulcerous feet, which made him unable to lend us aid, but he was none the less useful to me because, though he could not oversee the men at their labours, he could stay in camp to watch the goods, and to see that no skulkers were absent from duty.

This morning the men shouldered the goods and baggage and under Kacheche marched overland 3 miles to Zinga, while I resolved to attempt the passage down two small Falls, the Massesse and Massassa in the *Lady Alice* with the boat's crew. Clinging close to the shore, we rode down ¾ of a mile or thereabouts when we were halted by a lofty precipice, by the sides of which we could travel no further, as the tide, belched to right and left from the centre by the furious waters of the stream escaping down the Mowa Falls, came turning to meet us up river with many a brown wave and heave, and dangerous whirlpools. We then steered for the centre, and fought steadily on against the strong back tide, but it was of no use, and then we thought we would attempt the central stream that rushed with a white foamy face down river. Neither could we reach this, for the boat was heavy and sinking steadily under its growing weight of water, for she was very leaky and the repairs we had made were utterly insufficient.

By observing the shores and the more menacing appearance of the river, I perceived that instead of making any advance down river, we were imperceptibly being drawn towards the terrible whirling pools which almost momently play in the vicinity of the down stream and back tide, where the great waves heaved up by the raging and convulsive centre, and parting to right and left, are opposed by the back-tide flowing strong towards the fearful current.

Presently I saw at a little distance the first symptoms of the swirling vortex. Two floods flowing from different sides, with white brown crests, rush towards each other, the stronger raises its head, strikes and soon engulfs the weaker, which however dies not at once, but heaves upward convulsively, as if a volcano had suddenly burst beneath, into a watery hill which presently subsiding begins circling round with a small hole in the middle large enough for a garden dibble. This rapidly increases in volume, attracts or meets greater accession of force, until a terrible pool in appearance and form like a huge washbasin with the bottom knocked out – fatal to everything floatable that is near its verge or influence – whirling round like a flying wheel is found.

These were the symptoms which I saw, and as I saw the fatal watery pit though whirling still advancing, though advancing still whirling, the deathly snare whence if embraced was no escape, I shouted to oarsmen and steersman to do their best, or prepare to die. Meantime I threw off my coat and belts, and prepared for the worst. The oars bent under the sturdy efforts as though they would break, but in a few seconds we looked at the pit just over our stern, and a kindly wave near the verge of it drifted us further off. The boat by this time was half full of water, and I gave it up as an impossible task and returned to camp to try my luck in a canoe.

When I came to camp, the men left there were not sufficient to man a canoe, and I was compelled to proceed overland after the goods, not before telling my Captain, Manwa Sera, to send a rescue canoe with long cords to Zinga, where just below the Massassa Falls it might lie ready to lend a helping hand in case of accident. I talked with Frank before setting out about the difficulty, but that with great care and clinging close to the land with hauling ropes, the journey might easily be done by water.

In the afternoon I sat on the rocks of Zinga looking up river with field-glass in hand, and after long waiting I saw a canoe upset with 8 heads above water. Kacheche and Wadi Rehani were at once sent along the rocks to render any possible aid. Meanwhile I watched the men in the water, as they were borne into the basin of Bolo-Bolo by the spreading current. I saw their struggles to right her, I saw them raise themselves on the keel of the canoe and paddling. Finally I saw them land, but the canoe was swept down river over the Zinga Falls, then over the Ingulufi Falls, then away out of sight.

Bad news travels fast. I soon heard the names of the saved and those of the drowned. Among the latter was Frank Pocock, my servant, my companion and good friend.

Alas, my brave, honest, kindly-natured, good Frank, thy many faithful services to me have only found thee a grave in the wild waters of the Congo. Thy many years of travel and toil and danger borne so cheerfully have been but ill-rewarded. Thou Noble Son of Nature, would that I could have suffered instead of thee for I am weary, Oh so weary of this constant tale of woes and death; and thy cheerful society, the influence of thy brave smile, the utterance of thy courageous heart I shall lack, and because I lack, I shall weep for my dear lost friend.

'And weep the more because I weep in vain.'

It appears from the statements of the men and Uledi the Coxswain of the *Lady Alice*, that Frank, perceiving the rescue canoe about setting out, said that he could not wait for a second canoe but would go with the first, and accordingly took his seat and gave the word to set out. The strong back tide against which we had laboured in the morning proved no obstacle to them, for their vessel was swift and well manned. Two miles brought them to the cove between Massesse Falls and Massassa Falls, where the Coxswain told Frank it would be better to land on the rocks and examine the Falls first. Frank assented and sent him and three others to report on it. He was unable to proceed himself as he was troubled with ulcers in the feet.

The men after a long examination said it was a very bad place, that it would be a difficult job to go through. – 'Well, what shall I do, I am hungry, and I can't go by land. Must I die here from hunger? You people are so afraid of water that the slightest ripple makes you tremble. Where is the danger of going down the middle stream?' Frank consulting with his men thought there would be no danger by attempting the middle passage and by that road they set off without one presentiment or fear because they were all expert swimmers and divers, and Frank especially excelled in swimming and had often exhibited clever feats in that art, and to their minds Massassa Falls presented no difficulty compared with the many they had hardily passed.

They soon reached the glassy slope of the middle passage and had cleared the fierce yellow waves that seemed to chase them, but here the coxswain thought he would leave midstream and strike for the rocky precipice that lifts its brown front of solid rock a thousand feet into the air above the Bolo-Bolo Basin, and it was at the confluence of the down and back tide that Frank and two of my men met their Fate. The two water forces were just then meeting, they raised their foamy heads and dashed against each madly, and both after this first conflict embraced and subsided and in place of the liquid mound a pit was formed round the rim of which they were wheeled three or four times, during which time Frank tore his shirt off and all prepared for the deadly struggle. The bow of the canoe approached the middle of the pit, was sucked in and every soul was drawn down, down, down until – the survivors said – they thought their breasts would burst from the pent up air within, but after a few seconds the whirlpool relaxed its hold on their feet and they were soon ejected upward to see each other far apart, some saved, and some missing. Uledi and Wadi Baraka say they saw Frank twice above water senseless, the first of whom made a desperate effort to reach him with the tow rope, but it was too short. The two Wangwana they never saw. The most probable reason I can give of Frank's inability to save himself despite the weight of his clothes is that he must while struggling upward have struck his head against the canoe and become stunned; I am somewhat confirmed in this opinion from the fact that Wadi Baraka almost sank under the same canoe, but soon recovering regained hold and was saved.

At this place we first heard the distinctive titles of the Portuguese, English and French given, and wonder of wonders saw a jacket worn by one of the people.

The diaries go on to record his deep distress at the loss of his close friend, Frank Pocock, whose body was reported as having been seen but was not recovered. So the expedition pressed on, Stanley became ill with fever, the rapids tested them as always, and his own men now began to steal almost openly the very goods that would keep them alive. Without Pocock to watch over their positions, there was little Stanley could do to stop them. The work was continuously hard, food was in very short supply, and his men began to desert him. Nevertheless Stanley continued to battle against the river, navigating the few rapids he could and elsewhere laboriously portaging his boats overland. On 18 July he summarized the expedition to date, claiming to have attacked and destroyed twenty-eight large towns and up to eighty villages, fought thirty-two battles, and forced his way through or round fifty-two rapids or cataracts. He had constructed about thirty miles of rails, not unlike a tramway, through the forests and hauled his canoes and boats up at least one mountain 1500 feet high and then over mountains for a further six miles before lowering them down the steep slopes to the water's edge. He had lifted canoes over gigantic boulders up to seven metres in height and even built a type of tramway over these boulders.

He had also managed to obtain a fair amount of booty as a

result of his battles and states that he got $50 000 worth of ivory, 133 tusks and pieces of ivory, but had lost twelve canoes and thirteen lives. He had almost lost all the ivory and of course was always suffering from the thieving in his own camp. On 26 July one of his best captains, Wadi Safeni, went mad and disappeared. With starvation threatening and the local people far from friendly, and the river as bad as ever, the expedition continued until it reached another giant cataract at Isangila. This latest obstacle was far worse than anything he had seen before.

July 31st: Halt.

We had a visit from three Kings today, two of whom brought a goat each, a few peanuts and demijohn of palm wine, for which they received 3 *doti* each. The people are perfectly hateful to think of, with not one redeeming trait, insolent liars, poor and beggars. Here people sold addled eggs as chickens and wished to sell them 1 cloth each. We have decided to abandon the River as it is not in our power to continue the warfare longer. Tuckey's map is infamous for its errors and has been the prime cause of our fighting so long against natives.

So on 1 August 1877 Stanley left the river and started to march overland towards the Atlantic. A hundred years later the Zaire River Expedition still found the Isangila cataract a problem.

Wednesday 8 January

At 0825 hours boat party and Tac HQ advanced, climbing up on to the flat flood plain above the river. The first kilometre was easy going through cultivated fields. Then, after ten minutes' rest, we began to move through a difficult rocky area along the shore lines. Gradually the jungle that fringes the river got thicker, and soon we were slipping and sliding over the black rock. To add to our discomfort it began to rain, and in no time we were drenched to the skin as we pushed forward through the vegetation.

Fortunately, there were local pirogues on hand to take us across some of the small tributaries that flowed into the

river. The N'kenge River was the largest one we encountered. Here it took an hour to get personnel and porters
with their packs and equipment across the river, and we
lunched on the far bank. Rain continued, and as we grew
tired several of us suffered from falls. Kenneth Mason,
Daily Telegraph photographer, gashed open his arm, several
injured their backs and suffered bruises. Much more of this,
I thought, and we shall have a few broken bones. I did not
relish the thought of carrying casualties on this terrain. By
early afternoon we reached a bend in the river above the
Kianda Rapids. In an effort to attract the attention of Boat
Party A whom we fancied were just ahead, we fired a distress rocket. But as has often been the case, the rocket had
been affected by damp and only went fizzling for a few yards
from the end of the launcher. It nearly decapitated Mike
Gambier and Peter Marett who were standing close to me!

At last we reached the boat party on the beach near the
rapid at 1530 hours. The Avon recce boats had been lined
and portaged (only for 200 metres) past the rapids. Boat
Party A were ahead at the Lulu River. No airdrop arrived
this evening as requested, and our radio could not transmit
because of a fault. We did, however, hear that the Beaver
was held up and would drop to us first thing in the morning.
Very unfortunate, but an improvised meal of stew that
included, among other things, porridge and sardines, at
least filled our bellies and we spent an amusing evening
drying ourselves by the fire and exchanging songs with our
cheerful porters.

I noted many local pirogues along river and, especially
in calmer stretches, fishing is obviously a local industry.
Also saw four guinea-fowl, ibis and fish eagle. In one
tributary I noted a dead, four-foot water-snake. It had the
usual three double-white bands on neck at half-inch intervals, tail pointed and thin without a fin. Rocks on river
mixture of sedimentary and igneous.

Our sick continue to give rise for concern. Richard
Snailham has malaria and Basil Pratt, our chaplain, dysentery.

Thursday 9 January

The Beaver came in early this morning with mail. No food, but some was dropped ahead to Boat Party A at Lulu River. In my own mail were a host of problems and one more cheering item, a packet from my daughters enclosing some Christmas cake and peppermints. It was especially appreciated as breakfast was rather thin today.

I reckoned we should have to march about ten miles inland to reach Jim Masters' camp. As the sun rose, our long column wound its way up into green grass-covered hills. The sharp, pale-brown-coloured quartz rocks lacerated the feet of our porters and caused us to slip and stumble as we followed the narrow paths. Our guide warned us to beware of buffalo, both red and black variety. This was not encouraging as the only weapon we had with us, having left most of our arms in Kinshasa to save weight, was a signal pistol. Peter Marett had gone ahead to recce the route and joined us a few hours later with little good news. The march was going to be long and hard with many streams to cross. So we moved on through the midday sun, down slopes, across fast-flowing, crystal-clear streams, over slippery rocks, through fringing jungle, and back up the next slope.

At each crest I thought we must see the river, but somehow another valley and another crest always lay beyond. The river seemed to have deserted us. At 1330 hours we picked up Major Billy Bowles on our small Panasonic radio. He said he was just ahead but it was 1415 hours before our exhausted column reached him. On the beach we found food and water which were most welcome. Thereafter, we had a short march of a further three kilometres to Zodiac Bay. Here, on a sandy shore, we thanked and paid off our faithful porters who had done so well. They said they would stay the night, before returning to their village where they will doubtless tell the stories of their march for many years to come. The jets have gone, but the Avon recce boats should be able to reach the dam at Inga. We still have many rapids and much difficult country to overcome before we reach the sea, and so at dusk I set out with my Tac HQ to join the support group in Inga where Tom Mabe has kindly arranged an empty house as a base from which to plan the next move. Our sick could also be brought in and treated in shelter and reasonable comfort. Meanwhile, Tom must go ahead to brief local officials on our route to the Atlantic. On expeditions one neglects PR at one's peril!

Friday 10 January

This morning we moved the Avon recce boats to the edge of the dam at Inga. Thus we have succeeded in navigating the river with two of our different types of craft so far, for the jets reached here two days ago. The close recce section were in very fine spirits and as a reward for their endeavours I presented them with a bottle of J & B whisky, which in spite of the early hour they drained, neat, on the spot!

Now we must pause and prepare for the rest of the difficult way forward. I see little point in playing around in the actual complex of the dam as I believed we should simply be ridiculed for our pointless efforts. The water is extremely hazardous in this region and the conditions are rather artificial because much of the river had been obstructed by the spoil from the dam construction site. As a result of our reconnaissance, and in particular the efforts of Tom Mabe, I believe it would now be wise to launch the recce boat again a few kilometres away where a track reaches the river at a spot we call the Italian Beach. Marc Smith is very keen to attempt to get close to an enormous barrel-shaped wave that is almost static in the centre of the rapid after the dam. I have seen this from the air, and it is certainly an impressive stretch of water. A close-up photograph of this wave would be quite amazing. Peter Marett is going ahead to find the way to bring the giant boats in again below the Yalala Falls. However, there are twenty-three kilometres of river between Kanza and Yalala which I feel we should attempt to navigate. As we cannot safely get the giant craft around the Yalala Falls I believe this stretch should be left to the Avon recce boats.

Leaving Jim Masters and Marc to recce ahead, I flew in Beaver from Inga airstrip to examine water ahead. Using Polaroid cameras, we photographed these obstacles. I am of the opinion that the recce boats could get through from the Italian Beach to Yalala where we must portage for approximately one kilometre. A mistake above those falls would be certain death.

After dark I returned to Zodiac Beach to brief the boat crews on my decision and to launch the road-building operation to follow Peter's reconnaissance. Although the men are very tired they were eager to get on and the close recce section were delighted to be given the honour of navigating the sector between the Italian Beach and Yalala alone. I noted in my passage down-river in the dark that the recce boats did not have sufficient life-jackets for the passengers and crews, and accordingly I gave the crew a blasting.

Back at Tac HQ I noticed a certain amount of minor stress and strain between group commanders. Undoubtedly, now in the fourth month, there will be a certain amount of wear and tear on personalities.

Saturday 11 January

Early this morning there was another air reconnaissance to confirm that there was no way through the Yalala Falls except by warping and portage. I confirmed the final details for Operation Grampus, which is the code name for the road-building engineer task we are about to undertake. A major difficulty is my great shortage of transport. Still, I am better off than Stanley who only had men to carry his boats.

Mike Gambier went forward in a Land-Rover along the tracks to get as close as possible to the Yalala Falls and to carry out a detailed recce of this area on foot. Peter Marett reckons he has found a good route for the road within a thousand metres of the river, but it will take at least three days' back-breaking work in the growing heat. The latter part of the day was taken up in dealing with a mound of accumulated paper work, and I managed to write letters to our sick in Kinshasa and to those who have been evacuated to England. I believe is is important that all who have served us so faithfully and well should be kept in touch with developments in the field, and so we also sent out a news-letter, drafted by Richard Snailham, to other parties of the expedition who are scattered. Having selected Bill Coleridge to return early to England and make detailed arrangements for our reception on return, I gave him a written brief. In the afternoon I enjoyed a brief rest and talked to some of our sick who still include Basil Pratt and Richard Snailham. The day ended with an O group at 2030 hours.

Sunday 12 January

Operation Grampus launched. Out of the blue, two four-ton Mercedes army lorries arrived! These have been arranged by the senior LO, Captain Kayalo. What a godsend and just in time.

At 1400 hours Marc Smith and the close recce section ventured into the terrifying waters at the foot of Kanza Rapids. Positioned myself with TV and press photo-graphers on bank to photograph Marc's attempts to reach giant wave in centre of river. He edged his way skilfully forward along bank in Avon recce boat, using every ounce of power that the 40 hp Johnson engine would give. It was an outstanding performance and he got quite close to the great wave before being forced back by the driving spray and foaming water that was raging down the cataract. Need-less to say all men were in life-jackets, wet-suits and crash helmets. We are certainly learning much about the means of boating in near-impossible conditions.

FST/C has now been taken over by FST/A and the road-building has started in earnest. We have sent for explosive to crack through some large rocks at the far end of the road.

I am hopeful we can get through the final three rapids which are named Kisi 1, 2 and 3, but recent reconnaissance of Kisi 1 indicates that it will be no picnic! If we still had the jet craft with us I would feel more confident, but the die is now cast and we must stick by our decision.

Tom Mabe, our splendid American officer, has been ahead to the Atlantic, talking to officials and making arrangements for the final part of our journey.

Monday 13 January

No explosive arrived this morning. Tom Mabe is doing his utmost to get it, but naturally in a country such as this people are very suspicious about giving explosive away readily. However, the CIS (Inga Dam Construction Company) made six excellent crow-bars for us to use in shifting rocks.

After a one-and-a-half-hour drive, we reached the Yalala village and found the route forward clearly signed by Peter Marett. He really is an excellent intelligence officer. On reaching work site, found men were suffering from a great shortage of water and were now getting impatient to press on, for working in this heat is difficult. There is no water nearer than the river and that is a long four kilometres away downhill. However, the road is progressing well and will be completed on time. Tac HQ camp in the forest near Yalala village.

The camp site was well prepared by Lance-Corporal Peter Rose who has his radio station nearby and will work with us for the next few days.

News from rest of expedition indicates there has been a small electrical fire in Beaver. Although not serious, this is going to put it out of action for a short while at a time when I can least afford it. It will certainly affect the move of one of our scientists, Sinclair Dunnet, to Lisala where he hoped to find his elusive pygmy chimpanzee.

Villagers here very kind and brought fruit to us tonight. We exchanged gifts and found that many of them are Angolans, refugees from the fighting across the river. Already we have employed some sixty of them to help with the road.

Tuesday 14 January

Another scorching day. The two Zaire army drivers are doing well and go on non-stop, bringing forward our stores from Inga to the road. They were up early with their two Mercedes lorries, which seem to be first-class vehicles for use by an army. The giant inflatables were brought forward from Dick Festorazzi's store, neatly folded and prepared for the portage down to the river. On reaching the road-head nearest to the river we found that it was extremely difficult to move the boats down the boulder-strewn slope. We tried them both deflated and inflated, but it was hard work in blistering heat. Porters did an outstanding job and I have rarely seen men work so cheerfully under such adverse conditions. The whole event was well covered by the Survival–Anglia TV team and by Ken Mason for *The Daily Telegraph*. Meanwhile, the Avon recce boats were portaged around Yalala by Mike Gambier's group. Derek Jackson came up for a conference and also lent his back to shifting the boats. After lunch he returned to Inga for more stores and mail, and to dispatch film and pictures.

News from outside was not particularly encouraging. We had asked for a supply of balsa wood from London to help us construct a model boat as a gift for President Mobutu. Apparently, so the signal said, no balsa wood could be obtained in London! However, there was word of good coverage in *The Daily Telegraph* on 11 and 13 January. This is excellent for our men's morale, for undoubtedly there are times when they feel like a forgotten army. In the late afternoon we went in to Inga to collect the explosive which was now ready. It was in an extremely dangerous condition, and had it not already been drawn from the magazine I would have hesitated about carrying it back on the rough track to the river. But that was what we had to do, and together with Pam Baker and Ken Mason I drove very slowly back to the road-head bearing the lethal cargo. It was a journey reminiscent of the film, *The Wages of Fear*!

Wednesday 15 January

During the night we had tremendous thunder, lightning and heavy rain. The day was much cooler. While work was finishing off on road, I took party to visit Stanley's original station and base at Vivi which was some fourteen kilometres down-river. We went by vehicle at approximately 1000 hours and saw the partially reconstucted building. Villagers greeted us with political songs, and eventually we got to the house. There were a few prints and pictures and a plaque on the door saying, 'Touring Club de Belge-Congo 1958 – Sir H. M. Stanley'. It was a two-storey building with a few exhibits, and some old wheels which I reckon Stanley probably used to move boats on his return journey a few years later.

At Tac HQ we found some newcomers, including Maggie Bush and Dr Viv Jones, who had arrived from Kinshasa. The petrol for the boats had also arrived. Another flood of letters complaining about one or two of our ill-behaved members in Kinshasa. The explosive is in an even more dangerous state and we will have to destroy it tomorrow if we do not use it on the road.

Thursday 16 January

Early this morning we got rid of the dangerous explosive and moved a few rocks at the same time, largely for the benefit of television and press photographers! It was extremely unstable and unsafe.

One of the Zaire Army vehicles was damaged accidentally

when it struck a tree overhanging the narrow track. There is growing concern about the force of water in Kisi 1. Derek Jackson came forward to join me at Tac HQ for the short journey downriver.

Friday 17 January

Moved early to beach where I noted surges of up to one metre. Airdrop and air recce this morning confirm that Kisi is getting worse; now reckoned by Tom Mabe to be Grade 8 and almost suicidal. There is much concern, but I am confident that with care we can get through. The boats were carefully balanced under Jim Masters' watchful eye, and we arranged with the support group to resupply us at Matadi. The boats did not have outrigger pontoons fitted, simply because of the effort needed to get these items to the beach. I consider it would have been more prudent to use them, but everyone was eager to press on.

Our starting point was at the foot of the great Yalala Falls a most impressive sight as befits easily the worst rapids and waterfalls we have encountered in the whole of our journey. We have now observed them at both high and medium level river conditions, and they never look any less formidable. I doubt if they will ever be passable, though perhaps something might be done with a larger and more powerful boat. But then, after the Inga Dam is completed in 1984 there will be no point to further navigation on this stretch of the river.

We moved off into Kisi 1 at 1100 hours. All the skippers had done a land recce beforehand and knew the way we meant to tackle this last great challenge, but with so inconsistent a river no one could be really sure how this would work out. I was aboard La Vision who edged her way down first of all. Moving as cautiously as possible, we inched towards the line of tossing white water that rose from the surface. Suddenly we were confronted by the familiar tongue and V-shape formation of waves. We gently rolled over two lines of these, and then faced a series of crests of wild water in mid-channel. Our speed accelerated rapidly, rocks, boulders and the walls of the gorge flashed past with incredible speed. We all hung on for dear life as the brown water foamed over the bow of our bucking, articulating craft. The engine rose and fell as the helmsman controlled our passage. A whirlpool sucked at us in the tail of the cataract. One monster wave hit us, knocking us sideways for a few seconds before the helmsman regained control, and then we were through, spinning over to the right bank to deposit one of the TV teams before crossing through the racing current once again and into slack water in the lee of some rocks. From this position, using the Panasonic radio, I controlled the move down of the remaining craft.

The first to come through was *Barclays Bank*, which met with little difficulty. We then signalled the recce boats to try to negotiate a channel behind an island on the left side of the river. While attempting to do this, the leading recce boat was hit by a freak wave and capsized. From behind the island we in *La Vision* saw the red distress flare curve up into the sky. The boat's radio had gone dead and we feared the worst. Felt hairs rising on the back of my head; so the river had one last trick up its sleeve. All radio stations at their various points around the rapid reported that they could see nothing. By sheer ill-luck the accident had happened in the one dead spot that none of us could see, but it seemed the capsized recce boat, with its crew of three hanging on, had been quickly swept into the periphery of a giant whirlpool. We all knew only too well what would happen to a man, even wearing a life-jacket, if he were to go down in the yawning vortex.

Fortunately, however, the second recce boat, some hundred metres behind, *had* seen the plight of its sister craft and immediately went forward to the rescue, bravely helmed by Corporal Neil Rickard of the Royal Marines.[1] The waves

1. For this, Corporal Rickard was later awarded the Queen's Gallantry Medal.

between the two craft were formidable and it was with great courage that the crew of the second managed to get into this extremely dangerous area and pick up the three men from the very sides of the whirlpool. Hardly had they done this when the capsized boat was sucked down, as if into the plug-hole of a giant bath. Then from *La Vision* at the bottom of the rapid we suddenly saw a recce boat bobbing up as if from nowhere. We realized afterwards that it must have been driven along under water for approximately 1000 metres by the force of the current. *La Vision* moved forward and was able to secure the craft. Although somewhat damaged and with a certain amount of equipment missing, the boat was righted and made habitable once again. A spare engine was then put aboard and it was back in action. Having reorganized, we then ran down without much incident through Kisi 2 and Kisi 3.

The Atlantic seaport of Zaire, Matadi, came around the corner as we crossed the final rapid. It was indeed a great moment, and with a shower of Very lights we headed across the river to the ferry site where our support group waited with bottles of beer to greet us. After a brief refuelling stop we sailed on, camping for the night some thirty-six kilometres from Boma where we had heard a greater reception awaited us.

Hardly had our camp been set up when the sky darkened and the thunder began to roll. This it did throughout the night, to and fro, up and down the river. The rain came driving in squalls, soaking us to the skin, and the black sky shut out even the sunset. The elements seemed to moan and groan and grumble, and the boats rose and fell uneasily at the moorings on the shore as the surges came in. The river was fighting to the end like a dying beast. I wonder as I write this, does she begrudge us our victory? Or does she realize that no one will ever truly conquer her. I feel it is enough to have reached the Atlantic, and to have survived the rigours of this journey with all our men and most of our boats in one piece.

Saturday 18 January

Started fairly early in the day and had an easy run in bright sunshine to Boma where we were overwhelmed with hospitality provided by local officials and the Bralima brewery. A big party had been arranged at a local hotel in the evening, and there as guests of the brewery we enjoyed ourselves no end.

While in the town the Commissaire took us to an enormous hollow baobab tree. It is alleged that Stanley spent a night inside the hollow and later carved his initials on the trunk. There are a great many HMS initials all over the tree, and these are just souvenirs of later visits by British warships. We were assured, however, that the genuine initials were still to be found but now much higher up the trunk as the tree had grown considerably in the last hundred years.

We are now faced with the final run to Banana which will begin in the morning. Already there is a relaxed feeling, but one finds it hard to imagine that there isn't some secret rapid that we know nothing about. In fact, we had heard that an enormous whirlpool, feared even by ships, existed near Matadi. But we encountered nothing in our passage today.

Sunday 19 January

On to Banana. Before leaving we had a parachute drop into the river, mainly for television purposes. Waving farewell to our friends at Boma, we proceeded down-river in convoy and were soon faced with a hazard that we last experienced on the long haul between Kisangani and Kinshasa. The sea became turbulent and we faced quite large waves which made our journey both slow and wet. At 1500 hours we made radio contact with our advanced, overland party at Banana.

At 1600 hours we entered the basin of the Yacht Club at the port of Banana. A huge crowd had gathered and we were treated to one of the finest displays of dancing that we had seen on the whole expedition. The girls in colourful brassières and grass skirts performed their dances in front of a hut where we sat with the government officials and senior military officers of the garrison. As evening approached, we boarded our fleet and, together with our local friends, sailed out into the setting sun. Unfortunately, a large cargo vessel had anchored itself in the way of the sunset and so we had to sail for approximately two miles out to sea to get the setting sun in the right position! Having finally achieved this our chaplain, Basil Pratt, held a short service of thanksgiving. The TV and press boys then had an absolute ball, and it was dark before we returned towards the shore midst a shower of rockets and flares that we no longer had any use for. Fuel almost ran out on the way in, and with no lights we had quite a tricky passage reaching the dock again. And so it was over; the journey that had started so many months ago, and over 2700 miles upriver, was completed. We all felt too exhausted to do much celebrating and after a short speech[1] to the members, I retired to the Mangrove Hotel where the Commissaire had kindly arranged to put a few of us up. A delightful dinner followed and a small informal party.

Stanley's own journey ended rather differently.

August 1st: Leave river, boat and canoes start overland, and reach at noon 7 miles Ndambi Mbongo.

August 2nd: March 8 miles and camp in wilderness.

Tough work over mountains. Terribly hungry. I fear for my people. Beads are almost useless, brass wire not in demand, nothing but cloth of which we have so little that it is like the widow's cruse of oil. Stones troublesome.

August 4th: Halt.

Send Kacheche, Robert, Uledi, the Coxswain and Muini Pembe to Embomma with guides and letters to English and French traders, praying for relief in the shape of rice, grain, or cloth.

1. See Appendix A.

People out all over the country exploring for food; the baobab, calabashes and any edible roots. One peck of potatoes costs 4 yards of cloth; beads and shells or wine of not much value here, the cloth is so plentiful that it is almost worthless.

Palm wine is abundant but for hungry men something more substantial is needed.

August 5th: March to Mbinda 12 miles, a district of 16 or 17 villages. On the highest range crossed, Aneroid showed 2,100 ft. People amiable but terribly extortionate, and so keen in trading that my people get more and more emaciated.

These people are given up to the delights of palm wine and marketing women slaves, raise peanuts and a few potatoes etc. They are so lazy, that the country is almost inexplorable from the difficulty of procuring provisions.

August 6th: March to Banza Mbuko 4 miles. A market was close by and I heard that cowries were in demand and I instantly gave 40 to each man to procure food.

August 7th: March to N'lamba N'lamba 5 miles.

Soon after camping, Kacheche came with supplies. 5 gallons of Rum. 4 sacks of rice, 2 sacks of potatoes. 1 bag of tobacco. 3 large loads of fish and 1 load of sundry small things for myself such as tea, sugar, bread, butter, jam, fruit in tins, English shag and cigarette paper and 3 bottles of India Pale-Ale. The men gave three hearty cheers and a [*tiger?*] at the sight. The skeletonized men began to revive and this afternoon there is not a soul but is joyful. The long war against famine is over.

So Stanley marched on, finally reaching Embomma (Boma) on 9 August 1877. It was 999 days since the Anglo-American expedition had started out from Zanzibar. Almost a hundred years later the scene was slightly different. The Zaire River Expedition Log records:

Monday 20 January

This morning I returned to Kinshasa early by Beaver. There, we were greeted by masses of congratulations and one from President Mobutu. In the afternoon a signal was received from Britain which read:

From: Her Majesty the Queen, Buckingham Palace.
For: Lieutenant-Colonel[1] J. N. Blashford-Snell.

I am delighted to hear that the Zaire River Expedition has completed its task successfully. Please convey my warm congratulations to all members of the expedition on this notable achievement.

Signed:

Elizabeth R.

At this point I closed the official log of the expedition, but the generosity and hospitality of the Zaire Army, government and people was to continue. President Mobutu kindly sent his private 737 jet airliner to Banana to collect the boat teams and fly them back to Kinshasa. Zaire Army lorries moved our equipment. The President himself received us at a wonderful ceremony at the Presidency on Sunday 26 January. We were able to present him with a few simple gifts and invite him to join the Scientific Exploration Society. He accepted our invitation and made one request of us, 'When you go home to your countries, don't just tell your wives and your children but tell everyone about the hospitality that you have received here. We are a country that is often misunderstood, we want people to understand us.'

And most of us who stood that day looking out across the Great Kinsuka Rapids, on what had once been called Mount Stanley, vowed that we would do our utmost to help people to understand this man and his country.

[1]For the duration of the expedition, the author was given the rank of Local Lieutenant-Colonel.

Appendix A

Speech by Lieutenant-Colonel J. N. Blashford-Snell to members of the Zaire River Expedition on reaching the Atlantic at Banana, 19 January 1975

Tonight we have accomplished our mission in navigating as much as possible of this mighty river and carrying out important scientific and medical research en route.

Together we have faced and overcome many problems. The logistic support group have achieved an administrative miracle in solving our resupply and communication difficulties. Our boats' crews have overcome some of the most formidable rapids in the world and have survived many a capsize and even a hippo attack.

Our medical team have done a splendid job in keeping us all as fit as possible and although over the period of the expedition half of us became casualties I am happily relieved that we have lost no lives.

The lack of finance and the great problems of transportation in Zaire has been overcome by our support group and our friends in the Zaire armed forces.

Sometimes the problems have been within ourselves. There has been some strain, some frustration and disappointments, and some moments of great danger. Some of us have been thoughtless, selfishly putting their own needs before those of the whole expedition, others have been intolerant. But most of you have been utterly selfless and worked tirelessly. Furthermore I am sure you will agree that some, especially our sick, have shown great courage.

We have all changed a little, for this expedition has brought out our strengths and our weaknesses. But although we may have had a few failures, the fact that we have today achieved our final aim shows that we have been able to pull together as a team, and it is the teamwork that in the end has led to success.

But we have achieved more than just completing an epic voyage. Our scientists are all well pleased with their results, and although some groups may have achieved more than others I have not heard of a single really serious failure in the scientific research. We have shown that it is possible to navigate the Zaire River in safety for over 2000 miles from Bukama to Isangila with one type of craft and almost all the remainder with other types of boat. Indeed a notable fact has been the success of our boats.

I also believe that in these dark days of world tension we have shown that people of many nations, inspired by a sense of adventure and with a healthy contempt for difficulties and danger, can come together to perform a worthwhile task. At the same time it has been suggested that perhaps at this time of economic stress and general despondency this expedition may be a flicker of light in a gloomy sky that will help to promote a deeper understanding and foster the bonds of friendship between the peoples of both sides of the Atlantic and those of Africa.

To launch and carry out such a massive project has taken four years' hard work. Indeed it would not have been possible without the help and encouragement of President Mobutu Seso Seko, the Zaire government and armed forces, as well as that of many Europeans living in Zaire. The support of the British and United States armed forces, the Scientific Exploration Society, the Explorers' Club, and the Gestetner Corporation has been invaluable. Nor must we forget our many sponsors and HQ Staff in Britain who have all played a vital and important role in the venture.

For my part I have probably been unfair, unkind and lacking in understanding to many of you. Nevertheless, I count myself privileged to have led such a team and I thank you all for your loyalty. But, I must remind you that when we return to Britain the work must continue. Our author must write the book, our reporter must prepare the magazine articles, the film must be edited, and our scientists have years of work to do on their research. My own small staff have the awful burden of preparing the final report and raising funds to pay all our bills. It is in this last task that we need the help of everyone.

What you have achieved as a team is now history and I only hope that the results of this expedition will be a lasting credit to you all and of real value to mankind.

Appendix B
Zaire River Expedition Sponsors

Abbott Laboratories Ltd
Agence Maritime Internationale SA
Airscrew Howden Ltd
Airwork Services Ltd
Air Zaire
Aladdin Industries Ltd
Allen and Hanburys Ltd
Ames Co Ltd
Anglia Television Ltd
Mr Walter Annenberg
Arena Sports Advertising
Armstrong Patents Co Ltd
Army Central Fund
Astell Laboratory Service Co
Astra Chemicals Ltd
Athenaeum Hotel (Oddenino's) Limited
Ault and Wiborg Paints Ltd
Avimo Ltd
Avis Rent-A-Car
Avon Inflatables Ltd

Babcock and Wilcox Ltd
Bakelite Xylonite Ltd
Baptist Missionary Society
Barclays Bank International Ltd
Barr and Stroud Ltd
E. P. Barrus Ltd
Batchelors Catering Supplies Ltd
Bayer Pharmaceuticals Ltd
BDH Chemicals Ltd
Beecham Research International

HMS *Belfast*
John Bell and Croyden
Benguela Railway Co
Bentalls Ltd
Berghaus Ltd
Binnie and Partners
Black and Decker Ltd
S. Boardman (Air Services) Ltd
Boehringer Ingelheim Ltd
Boots Co Ltd
Bow Marketing Ltd
Brasserie, Limonaderies et Malteries du Zaire
Brexton Ltd
Britax (London) Ltd
T. T. Broughton and Sons Ltd
British Aircraft Corporation Ltd
British American Tobacco Co Ltd
British Berkfeld Filters Ltd
British Caledonian Airways Ltd
British India Steam Navigation Co Ltd
British Oxygen Co Ltd
British Posters Ltd
The Brock Group of Companies
Brooke Bond Liebig Services Ltd
Brown Best and Co Ltd
David Brown Gear Industries Ltd
Sir Felix Brunner
Bryant and May Ltd
Buckmaster and Moore
Buckmaster School

Cadbury Schweppes Foods Ltd
James Capel and Co
Carreras Rothman
Champion Sparking Plug Co Ltd
Charter Consolidated Ltd
Ciba Laboratories
Cinema Products (Los Angeles)
Mr D. Coldridge
Collett, Dickenson, Pearce and
Partners Ltd
Mr W. Collings
Collins Bros (The Southern
Armoury) Ltd
Compagnie des Chemins de Fer
(Zaire)
Coopers Mechanical Joints Ltd
Mr C. H. Cossham
G. Costa & Co Ltd
Counsel Ltd
Coutts & Co
CPC (United Kingdom) Ltd
Curry and Paxton Ltd

Daily Telegraph
James Davey Sites Ltd
Davidson Radcliffe Group Ltd
DEB Chemical Proprietaries Ltd
Colonel Paul S. Deems
Desmo Ltd
His Grace The Duke of
Devonshire, PC, MC
John Dewar and Sons Ltd
Dome Laboratories
Down Bros & Mayer & Phelps
Ltd
Draper Tools Ltd
Alexander Duckham & Co Ltd
Mr Peter Duckworth
Dylon International Ltd

Lieutenant-General Sir John
Eldridge, KBE, CB, DSO, MC
Electronic Laboratories Ltd
Electronic Concepts Ltd

The English Speaking Union
(Norwich and Norfolk Board)
Mr R. F. Entwhistle
Erricks Photoshops
Eton College, Natural Science
Society
The Ever Ready Company (GB)
Ltd
Exeter School
The Explorers Club of New York

Fairey Winches Ltd
The Financial Times
Fleet Amenities and Fleet
Recreational Funds
Duncan Flochart & Co Ltd
Fosbery and Co Ltd
Foseco Minsep Ltd
Mr T. Fraser-Jones
French Gold Abbot Kenyon &
Eckhardt Ltd

The A. W. Gale Will Trust
Gallay Ltd
A. Gallenkamp and Co Ltd
Mr L. J. Galloway
Gardenwork (Solihull)
GEC-Elliott Mechanical
Handling Ltd
General Foods Ltd
Gestetner Duplicators Ltd
W. & A. Gilbey Ltd
Gillette Industries Ltd
GKN Group of Companies Ltd
Gladys Tompson Trust
Glaxo Laboratories Ltd
Glints of London Ltd
Sir Gerald Glover
F. Goddard and Co Ltd
Siebe Gorman and Co Ltd
Great Walstead Preparatory
School
Green Island Cement Co Ltd
H. S. Greenfield and Son
Gresham Lion Ltd

Hach Europe SA/NV
Hagman Laboratories (1933) London
Hamilton Jet (UK) Ltd
H. J. Heinz Co Ltd
Hoare and Company Covett Ltd
Hoechst Pharmaceuticals Ltd
Holland and Holland Ltd
P. H. Holt Charitable Trust
Holt Products Ltd
Homefield School, Rugby
Honda (UK) Ltd
Michael Hooker & Associates Ltd
Hunter Boats (Sales) Ltd
John A. Hunter Co Ltd
Hutchinson Publishing Group Ltd
Hyett Adams Ltd
Hyvision Ltd

Imperial Chemical Industries Ltd
Imperial Metal Industries (Kynoch) Ltd
Ingersoll Electronics Ltd
International Distillers and Vintners Export Ltd
Inzal (Zaire)
Mr Fred Irving

Jersey Wildlife Preservation Trust
C. J. Jonen Shipping Ltd
Justerini and Brooks Ltd

Keeler Instruments Ltd
Kemwell Ltd
The Kings School, Ely
Kiwi Polish Co Pty Ltd
Kleinwort, Benson Ltd

Laird (Anglesey) Ltd
Lakeview Trading Co SA

Lederle Laboratories Division (Cyanamid of Great Britain Ltd)
Link Travel
Sir Hugh Linstead
Mr J. L. Llewellyn
London and Provincial Poster Group Ltd
Joseph Lucas (Export) Ltd

Mabey and Johnson Ltd
Macdonald and Muir Ltd
Mrs R. A. Macpherson
Mr and Mrs Mamwell
Mariners Weigh
Marsavco (Zaire)
The Bob Martin Co
Martini and Rossi Ltd
Frank Mason and Co Ltd
Matheson and Co Ltd
May and Baker Ltd
MEL Equipment Co Ltd
Merck, Sharp and Dohme Ltd
Merrydown Wine Co Ltd
Mersea Sales and Service Ltd
The Metal Box Co Ltd
The Miles Group of Companies
Mintex Ltd
R. Mitchell and Co (Engineers) Ltd
Modern Maintenance Products Ltd (Tribol Ltd)
Moet and Chandon (London) Ltd
Molyslip Holdings Ltd
More O'Ferrall Ltd
Moss Bros Ltd
Munrospun Ltd

National Westminster Bank Ltd
Navy, Army and Air Force Institutes
The Nestlé Co Ltd
New Cheshire Salt Works Ltd

Nicholas Products Ltd
Nuffield Trust for Forces of the Crown

Mr Richard Oaten
Ocean Transport and Trading Ltd
Office Supplies Ltd
Orion Insurance Co Ltd

The Pacific Steam Navigation Co Ltd
Package Control Ltd
Pains-Wessex Ltd
Palitoy Ltd
Parke-Davis & Co
H. Parrot & Co Ltd
J. Payen Ltd
Penlon Ltd
Perkins Engines Group Ltd
Pfizer Ltd
Philips Industries
Pinchin Denny & Co
Pindisports
Polaroid (UK) Ltd
Portacal Ltd
Potter and Clarke Ltd
The Prestige Group Ltd
Mr C. Price
Proctor and Gamble Ltd
Pye Telecommunications Ltd

Quaker Oats Ltd

Racal Electronics Group
RAF Central Fund
The Rawlplug Co Ltd
Reckitt and Colman Products Ltd
Reuben Gaunt & Sons Ltd
Roche Products Ltd
Ronson Products Ltd
Roussel Laboratories Ltd
Rowe & Pitman Hurst Brown

The Royal Automobile Club
The Royal Scottish Geographical Society
The Royal Sovereign Group Ltd (Speedry Division)
The Royal Trust Co of Canada
RT Vehicles Ltd

Sabena Belgian World Airlines
St Peter's School, York
Salter and Varge Ltd
Samuel Lee-Bapty Ltd
Samuelsons Film Service
Schrader Automotive Products Division
Major General and Mrs T. Scott-Elliot
Scottish and Newcastle Breweries Ltd
G. D. Searle & Co Ltd
Joseph Sebag & Co
Sellotape Products UK
Shaftesbury Grammar School
C. Shippam Ltd
J. J. Silber Ltd
Simoniz
Sinclair Calculators
Major General Sir John Sinclair, KCMG, CB, OBE
Sony (UK) Ltd
South Western Marine Factors Ltd
Spanset Ltd
Speery Gyroscope
Miss C. Staddon
Standard and Chartered Banking Group Ltd
Stanley Tools Ltd
Stiefel Laboratories (UK) Ltd

Tandberg Radio Fabric AS
Tanganyika Concessions Ltd
Tate and Lyle Refineries Ltd
Mr J. M. Temple, JP, DL

Thermos Ltd
The Arthur Thomson
  Charitable Trust
Time for Watches and Jewellery
  (Jersey)
Tirfor Ltd
Toyota (GB) Ltd
Travenol Laboratories Ltd
Tri-Wall Containers Ltd
The Tupperware Co Ltd
Twyford School

United Africa Co Ltd
United Services Trustee
US Army

Van Ommeron (Zaire)

John Walker and Sons Ltd
Walker's Advertising Associates
  Ltd
B. J. Ward Ltd
Dr J. G. Watson

Mr P. G. Wedgwood
The Wellcome Foundation Ltd
Wessex Regional Health
  Authority
Whitby and Co
Wiggins Teape Paper Ltd
Williams and Glyn's Bank Ltd
W. D. & H. O. Wills
Wilwyn Animal Care Ltd
George Wimpey and Co Ltd
Winsor and Newton Ltd
Winthrop Laboratories
World Timer
The Worshipful Company of
  Drapers
The Worshipful Company of
  Skinners
Mrs A. Wrigley
Wrigley Co Ltd

Yardley International Ltd
Mr D. Young

Zyls Metal AG (Switzerland)